How
Do You Know
It's
OLD?

How
Do You Know
It's
OLD?

*A Practical Handbook on
the Detection of Fakes for the
Antique Collector and Curator*

by

Harold L. Peterson

CHARLES SCRIBNER'S SONS
New York

To
DONALD D. DONOHUE

who has fought the good fight

Library of Congress Cataloging in Publication Data

Peterson, Harold Leslie, 1922–
  How do you know it's old?

  Bibliography: p.
  1. Art objects—Collectors and collecting.
2. Collectors and collecting. I. Title.
NK1125.P435   745.1   74-13118
ISBN 0-684-13981-2

ACKNOWLEDGMENTS

Many friends and colleagues have generously helped in the preparation of this volume. They have offered advice and encouragement, made suggestions based on their own experiences, permitted or provided photographs of specimens in their possession. To all of these kind people I am deeply grateful:

T. S. Avery
Robert Bearnes
Howard L. Blackmore
Claude Blair
Charles F. Bridgman
J. Duncan Campbell
James F. Deetz
Stanley Diefenthal
John and Jane Diehl
Donald D. Donohue
Charles G. Dorman
Martha Gandy Fales
Norm Flayderman
James D. Forman
Ron A. Gibbs
Craddock R. Goins, Jr.
Per E. Guldbeck

Caroline J. Hadley
Donald W. Holst
Bruce King
Robert L. Klinger
Donald E. Kloster
Harold H. Lutiger
Robert H. McCauley, Jr.
Robert B. Mayo
John C. Milley
E. Andrew Mowbray
A. V. B. Norman
Ralph Sheetz
Joseph Peter Spang, III
Samuel Stetson
M. W. Thomas, Jr.
Kenneth M. Wilson

In addition, very special thanks are due two people. Bluford W. Muir, photographer extraordinary, labored long and hard under an amazing variety of conditions to obtain pictures that would illustrate this work. All of the photographs except those credited to specific museums or individuals are his work. My wife, Dorothy, typed the manuscript as she always does for my books. More important, however—she has never laughed when I have bought a fake!

FOREWORD

Si non errasset, fecerat ille minus

The student of antiques who says he has never been fooled just doesn't know it yet. This is my firm belief after almost half a century as a private collector and professional museum curator. A colleague once told me that the late Henry Francis du Pont, founder of the justly famed Winterthur Museum, had his doubts also. Having viewed a collection for the first time he would often say to his guide, "You've shown me your treasures. Now show me your fakes." It was an astute request, for the response would tell much about the honesty and intelligence of the collector. We all get taken at one time or another, but the ability to recognize it separates the true student from the dilettante. Every museum has its "Chamber of Horrors," and that includes Mr. du Pont's Winterthur. Only the unknowing or dishonest will claim they have never had any.

The chance that you will buy a fake is a fact of life. You should not fear it or refuse to collect because of it. Back in 1893 the great British archeologist Sir John Evans declared, "As dogs must pass through their distemper, so an antiquary must have bought his forgeries before he can be regarded as thoroughly seasoned." Only by gambling your money can you learn. No education is free, and the cost of a fake can be considered tuition—provided you learn by the experience.

There are ways to reduce this cost. Certainly there is no point in being fooled by a poor forgery. And there are ways to alleviate the sting once you realize you have been caught. These methods are the subject of this book.

Perhaps it would be wise here to define the word "fake" as I will use it in the ensuing chapters. Many authorities insist that an object cannot be a fake unless there is an intent to deceive, and they separate honest reproductions from purposeful forgeries. For my purposes I will dispense with that distinction. Many honest reproductions lose their identity with the passage of years and end up as purported originals without the slightest intent of fraud on any-one's part. To the ultimate buyer the intent makes no difference whatsoever. All he wants to know is whether the piece he pur-chases is actually as old as its form would lead him to believe. Thus I use the word "fake" loosely and arbitrarily throughout to cover anything that is not of the period it might appear to be.

With this in mind, let's consider some of the ways you can limit your acquisition of fakes to the very best of their kind and perhaps, in addition to the knowledge you will gain from recognizing them, salvage something from the experience. Whatever happens, don't be ashamed of discovering you have been fooled. You are in the very best of company.

Harold L. Peterson

Washington, D.C.

CONTENTS

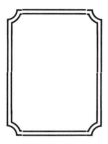

Introduction

Visitor: "What kind of a chair is that?"

Curator: "It's a Sheraton style side chair, made about 1800."

Visitor: "How do you know?"

Curator: "It follows the designs in Sheraton's book. Also the workmanship and materials are of the period."

Visitor: "But how do you know someone didn't follow that design, use the same materials and work in the same manner just a few years ago? *How do you know it's old?*"

For every museum curator, antique dealer and collector this conversation is repeated innumerable times throughout his career. Often he finds it impossible to answer. The little details that separate a genuine specimen from a more recent copy are hard to describe—and all too frequently they are unknown even to the person who has spent many years looking at antiques. The evidence is usually there, however. Every specialist has different ways of finding and recognizing it. In the following pages I hope to point out some of the things I have noticed in looking for authenticity in more than forty years of studying antiques.

First of all, let's get rid of some of the misapprehensions. Time and again people have told me: "I know this has to be old because of the circumstances under which I acquired it." The person who believes this can be badly fooled. Sometimes the circumstances of discovery can indeed be collateral evidence. But never be too sure. In this regard I have always liked the story that the late Bashford Dean, the great Curator of Arms and Armor of the Metropolitan Museum of Art, used to tell. On a visit to England many years ago Dean stopped in at a dilapidated village church. There, to his excited and covetous eye, hung a magnificent 14th century great helm over the tomb of its owner. It was dusty and covered with cobwebs, but Dean managed to have it taken down for a close look. Nothing would induce the church to sell it. The verger said so immediately, and he was backed by the vicar and the vestry. But the avid collector was not to be put off. The church badly needed repairs, and in a diplomatic move Dean agreed to pay for these if he could have the helm. Reluctantly the authorities agreed. Broke but elated, Dean carried the helm back to his hotel in London. He could hardly wait to call the young scholar Guy Laking to admire his treasure. The helmet lay on the bed as Laking entered and asked the whereabouts of the great discovery. "There," pointed Dean. "Oh, that!" said Laking. "That's from Saint So-and-So's. They've been trying to get rid of it ever since I can remember." Whereupon he knocked the treasure into pieces and exposed a recent product. For the rest of his life Dean kept the fraudulent helmet in his armory of magnificent specimens. It was, he said "for the good of my soul. I look at it whenever I feel I'm in danger of becoming too trustful!"

Another canard that many collectors cling to is the belief that "It couldn't be a fake. Nobody could spend all the time necessary to produce that and make any money." This opinion is far less believable than the first. For one thing it is often not the maker who sells the piece. It may be his widow or one of several succeeding owners who have no idea what was paid for the specimen in the first place. I am the proud owner of a "dog lock" musket with many mysterious alterations that I did not look at closely enough because it cost only $10 in a New England antique shop.

Figure 1 (right)
French musket model 1728 cleverly converted into a "dog lock". Since it was found in an obscure shop at a very low price, the buyer's suspicions were lulled.

Figure 2 (above)
The lock of the "dog lock" musket. The end of the screw at the very front of the lockplate has been slightly riveted to make it almost impossible to remove the lock and see the changes in the lock mortise. The dog catch for the cock is missing, and there is no pivot for it. Thus the lock does not belong to the gun and the cock does not belong to the rest of the lock.

Figure 3
Side plate of the "dog lock" musket. The very old looking screws are actually modern machine screws that have been artificially rusted.

Figure 4 (above)
Newly engraved dies for stamping the obverse and reverse of the reproduction Bermuda 3-penny coin. Since the maker was not trying to produce a fake he altered the shape of the mainsail. On the original coin it came down below the gunwale. He also worked his initial into the rigging. Still, one dishonest man tried to sell some of the coins stamped from these dies as originals. *Courtesy Robert L. Klinger.*

Figure 5 (below)
Obverse of the reproduced Bermuda "Somer Island" or "Hog" coins.

Figure 6
Reverse of the Bermuda coins.

Even twenty-five years ago this was very little money for such a piece, and my guard was down.

There are also an unbelievably large number of people who like to make things "just to fool the experts" or to see if they can make something in the old-fashioned way. One friend of mine made his own dies copying a set of 17th century Bermuda 2-, 3-, 6- and 12-penny coins to see if he could do it. He gave a few of his strikes to friends, only to discover that one had betrayed him and sold the new strikes as originals. My friend immediately destroyed the dies, but some damage had been done to unwary collectors—despite the fact that the die-maker had worked his initial "K" into the rigging of the ship that appears on one side of the coins.

Often reproductions are just plain deviltry, with no crass commercial thought of making money. Some twenty-five years ago a friend of mine purchased a cannon model that was purported by the dealer to be of 16th century origin. When the piece arrived the new owner noted immediately that the worm holes in the carriage were the size of a nr. 51 drill and that they went straight in and did not turn. This was bad enough, but the "rust" on the barrel turned out to be a mixture of rust and plastic wood. Naturally he sent the piece straight back to the dealer. He had not been fooled, but one of our group, a young cartridge collector, teased him unmercifully about having been hoodwinked. My friend decided to get even and prove that most people, including the cartridge collector, could indeed be hoodwinked in reality.

Night after night he labored in his basement workshop. On his lathe he turned a brass cartridge case the likes of which no one had ever seen before. Then he cast the bullet into the case so that it expanded behind the neck and could not be pulled out for further examination which would have revealed tell-tale drill or lathe marks. Finally he put false draw marks on the case to suggest it had been stamped and drawn, patinated it and dashed off to the home of a woman who had recently found a box of cartridges among her deceased husband's effects and which she planned to give to the young collector. Having secreted the new cartridge in this box my friend returned home to await results. They were spectacular. The collector was completely taken in. He sent photographs to other collectors all over the world to try to identify it, and it was only by dint of fast footwork and an X-ray that my friend kept it out of a standard book on cartridges. The joke had gotten so far out of hand that it had become next to impossible to stop it.

Things can get even further out of hand. Back in the 1920's a famous collector of Colt and other firearms became irritated by an acquaintance who always claimed to know it all. No matter what anyone showed him he could tell him all about it. Thus the Colt collector and a friend decided to teach him a lesson. They took a standard model 1851 Colt navy revolver which was made with an octagonal barrel. Colts were cheaper then so they put the barrel on a lathe and turned it round. The next time the "know-it-all" appeared they showed their revolver with its new round barrel to him, and sure enough he had a long story about what it was and its rarity. They ended up trading it to him for a couple of other guns, and he left delighted. A week later they called on him, explained the joke and offered him his guns back. To their surprise, his reaction was "Oh, no, you don't! You've just found out how valuable this piece is and want it back!" He refused to return the specimen and clung to his belief in it. It is now illustrated as a rare variation in a well-known history of the Colt revolver. A complete fraud that no one made money on is now immortalized in print!

So much for criteria you cannot use to determine the authenticity of a specimen. What are the real clues? Basically they revolve around design and construction—is the piece in proper design for the period; is it made in the proper fashion with the proper tools and fastenings; is it made of the proper materials and does it show the proper signs of aging and use?

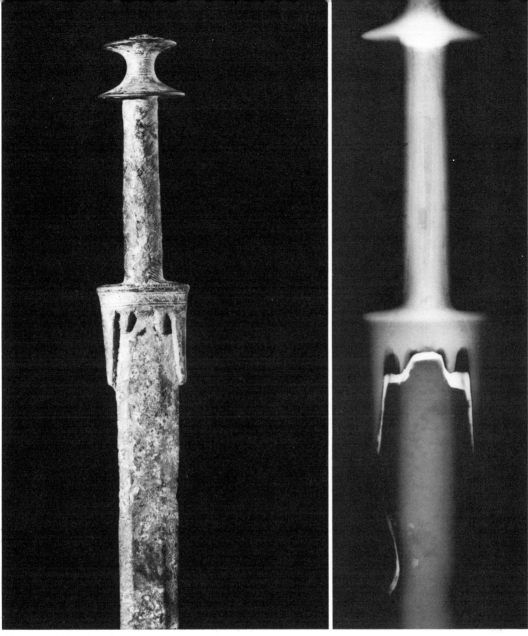

Figure 7 (above left)
Bronze sword from Iran recently purchased by a collector in New York.
Visually the patina matches throughout, and the piece appears homogeneous.
Courtesy C. F. Bridgman, Eastman Kodak Company.

Figure 8
Radiograph of the same sword that clearly shows a solder line (white)
between the blade and hilt indicating that parts from two swords have been
put together in modern times. The joint had been covered with paint and
sand to conceal it. *Courtesy C. F. Bridgman, Eastman Kodak Company.*

No handbook of this size is going to teach you styles. I will mention aberrations from time to time, but I assume that you already know the difference between Queen Anne and Art Nouveau and would be shocked to find the two combined. Workmanship will be covered in slightly more detail, but the main thrust of my comments will be on how materials age and wear. These are the most difficult things to fake properly, and I'm afraid they are the ones most often overlooked by the average collector. True, not every object has seen hard use. Its wear may be minimal, but if it is old it has aged, and it will have picked up some of the characteristics that come with time.

Figure 9 (top)
Inexpensive magnifiers come in a variety of shapes, sizes and powers. The glass with the flashlight handle and the black rectangular model in the left center both have battery powered lights which make them very useful in dark shops.

Figure 10
Ultra-violet lights can be obtained in a number of different strengths and designs. This simple and inexpensive unit will perform most of the tasks the average collector demands of it.

Tools of the Trade

Myths abound, but basically there are only three necessary tools for detecting objects that are newer than they appear at first glance. And these are all in your head. First is a keen set of eyes, second a good memory, and third a knowledge of what to look for.

Laymen are always impressed with newspaper accounts of scientific detection devices used by museums. There are one or two tools you can acquire that will be of help, but most of the stories deal with instruments and techniques that would be utterly impractical or useless for the decorative arts field in the periods which most people collect. Take the famed Carbon-14 test, for instance. In the first place it has a 200-year margin of error. To be useful it must be used only for objects of great antiquity in which this error would be unimportant. It certainly would be of no use on a Chippendale chair since it would be exceedingly important to know precisely whether it was made in 1750 or 1950. Also it is a very expensive test, and one has to wait a long time to get his sample tested—far longer than any dealer in his right mind would hold an average piece "on approval," even if he let you cut off the sliver for analysis. Much the same comments apply to the use of thermoluminescence, which works on glass obsidian and other minerals that have been heated and exposed to light and measures the time that has elapsed since exposure. And there are other techniques, such as those that record the magnetic orientation of ceramics. These tests work fine on such things as the skull of Piltdown Man, which turned out to date within the last two hundred years rather than thousands of years ago. But collectors of objects made since the Renaissance will find these methods of curiosity interest only.

There are some scientific techniques that are marginally useful to the average collector or small museum curator, especially if he is contemplating the purchase of an expensive or important piece. These include radiography and spectrographic analysis. A radiograph can detect many interesting things. It can show up even the cleverest weld or solder joint. It can demonstrate the presence of core structures or other items that should not be present inside certain specimens—and, for those collectors of historic ordnance who worry about the safety of their families and friends, it can show whether a shell is loaded and the exact condition of the fuse. Fortunately, collectors and curators of museums without radiographic facilities can often obtain these services. Every city and many towns have a radiographer who serves the local physicians. Depending upon the personality of the individuals concerned, these worthies can sometimes be persuaded to interrupt their happy pursuit of barium and use their equipment for your purposes—for a sufficient fee. Some cities boast regular industrial radiographic laboratories, and these are even better. The cost, however, is always such that these expedients should only be pursued on relatively expensive objects.

Another scientific technique of value to collectors of the decorative arts is the spectrographic analysis of metal. This is especially important to collectors of silver and classical bronzes. Again, there is considerable cost. But if you are contemplating the expenditure of several thousand dollars on the purchase of an American silver tankard it is only wise to seek the advice of another expert, hopefully one from a major museum who might be able to have the spectrographic analysis made at his facility "for his own information."

Now to the tools I think every collector and curator should have. Again, there are three. First is a set of magnifying glasses, second a strong light source, and third an ultra-violet light. Fortunately none of these is expensive and none need take up much space.

The choice of magnifying equipment is largely personal. There are all sort of devices on the market, and each has its supporters. Some like a jeweler's loop with a headband or attachment for one's eye glasses, and high magnification. It is very convenient, holding the glass in a fixed position and allowing free movement of both hands. There are also binocular lenses in the same styles which permit the use of both eyes. Some use a lighted glass with a handle holding flashlight batteries. It allows use under less than ideal lighting conditions. Both of these devices are bulky, however, and difficult to carry around to shops, but there is a new 5× magnifier with tiny batteries and light which fits easily into a pocket or purse. There are also electrically lighted magnifiers on mounts for use at home which are very handy. Personally, I like to have two glasses with me whenever possible. One is a fairly low-power glass with a relatively large field. The other is a small set of three lenses, less than an inch across. Usually these come in 5× to 20× and can be used singly or in combination. With these one can judge tool marks, abrasions, etching, patina and the pitting in crevices and especially, in the walls of crevices. More about this in the discussion of metal objects. Generally speaking, the lower the magnfication you can use the easier it is to handle because of the greater depth of focus. High magnification requires precise holding and considerable practice.

A good strong but small light source, perhaps a Tensor, allows the use of raking light on a surface. This shows up tool marks and abrasions, dips where the surface has been removed for whatever purpose, and so on. It is almost a must for furniture study, for some ceramics, and is useful even for metals.

Finally, there is the ultra-violet light. Many scientific and art firms manufacture these in a number of forms. The simplest just has a light tube in a metal holder on the end of an extension cord. The most elaborate operates either from batteries in a flashlight-type handle or hooked to household electricity, whichever is more convenient. The former, of course, is far better for carrying around to shops and saves one from asking the proprietor if he can plug into his current to examine one of his specimens. These lights quickly show any use of pigment or glaze other than the original on ceramics or painted tin. Each pigment fluoresces differently, and the newer pigments will usually appear black. A black splotch or an area of a different color on the plain bottom of a cup will immediately raise suspicion that the name of a country or origin has been removed and an artificial glaze painted over the spot to make it seem older. Lead glass and soda glass fluoresce as different colors. There are dozens of other uses as well. These are discussed in the sections on horn and ceramics.

Basically, however, all this recommended equipment is nothing more than an aid to the eye. As I said in the opening statement, the eye, memory and knowledge are the most useful tools of all connoisseurs, and to these the rest of this manual will be addressed.

Figure 11

Portion of the back of a 17th century English oak chest. The panel in the center has shrunk so much that it has pulled completely free of the stile on the left. This picture also illustrates the textures one should expect to find on wood that has been split or cut with a pit saw. Also noteworthy are the protruding pegs above and below the stile at the right, the replaced hinge at the top, and, a little to the left, the hole from the original cotterpin (staple) hinge.

Figure 12

The top of a 17th century German chest of painted spruce. Because the panels could not pull out of the frames as they shrank they have split.

Figure 13 (right)
Detail of the inside of the German chest lid. One of the splits caused by shrinkage appears at the bottom. Another evidence of age shrinkage (as well as of the originality of the hinge) can be seen to the right of the hinge finial. As the wood shrank it pulled away from the hinge and exposed a small area that has patinated lighter than the rest of the lid because it has not been exposed quite so long.

Figure 14
The knuckle of the arm of a windsor chair. Note how long use has worn the original black paint off the high spots and also how the wooden peg that helps hold the two pieces of the arm together protrudes because of the shrinkage of the arm. It is visible on the low line of the arm just behind the knuckle. The circular area at the right is the top of the front arm support. Different shrinkage patterns have caused the paint to crack around it.

2 Wood

Wood is a wonderful material for the student who wants to judge the age of an antique. For one thing, it shrinks with age. For another, it is relatively soft. It holds tool marks; it scars; it wears away with use and it discolors with age. Every one of these characteristics provides a clue to the person who knows how and where to look.

Like every other form of organic substance, newly cut wood contains a considerable amount of moisture when it is removed from a living tree. As soon as it is cut the moisture starts to evaporate, and this causes shrinkage. Much of this shrinkage occurs during the seasoning period when the green timber is left to become sufficiently stable for use. But the cabinet maker or treen worker does not wait until all the moisture is gone. This would take decades. Shrinkage, therefore, continues for years after the wood has been fashioned into a useful object or piece of furniture. The fibers which form the grain shorten very slightly, almost negligibly. Most of the dimensional changes occur across the grain as the fibers contract in diameter. The dense hard woods such as mahogany, maple, oak and walnut shrink very little. The softer varieties such as pine, poplar, and spruce change size enough to present visible differences to the naked eye.

The trained curator or collector is very conscious of these

dimensional alterations, and he looks for evidence that they have taken place. One of the most obvious places to look is a section turned on a lathe which would have been nearly perfectly round when made. If it is still round, the student knows it has not been turned very long. He may need calipers to detect the fact that the columnar support of a maple candle stand is out of round, but a good eye or at most a sensitive hand will reveal this condition in a pine table. The same thing is true of a turned treen plate or bowl —unless the maker used burl where the grain is so tangled that shrinkage is hard to see.

Age shrinkage becomes apparent in many less obvious ways as well. Panels will constrict across the grain. The early makers of furniture knew this well, so they usually set their panels in frames grooved deeply for the panel to shrink the anticipated amount without pulling completely out of the frame. They also frequently stained the whole panel before putting it in its frame so that shrinkage would not reveal unfinished wood. Since shrinkage is directly related to overall area, they usually kept the panels relatively small. Good examples of this can be found in 17th century chests. Even English oak which shrinks less than softer woods will reveal a narrow area along one or both sides of its panels that is patinated a lighter color than the rest because it has not been exposed to the air as long. Sometimes, when the maker has failed to anticipate the full amount of shrinkage that would take place in three centuries—plus the unforeseen drying caused by central heating—one can actually see the edge of a panel that has pulled free. If the original maker or a later restorer made the mistake of fastening the panels rigidly in their grooves so that they could not contract, the force of the shrinkage is so great that the panels will split. This may be unsightly, but it is a good sign of age and authenticity. Additional places where panel shrinkage is easily seen include cupboard doors and the ends of sleigh beds.

In other forms of case furniture, the effects of shrinkage are most easily observed in drawers. Drawer bottoms are almost al-

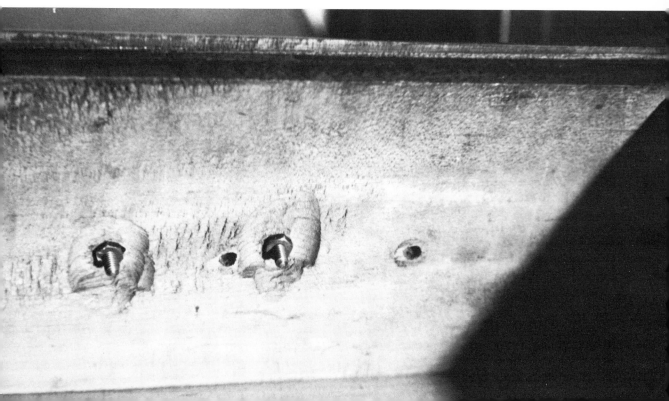

Figure 15 (above)
Profile of the side of a drawer showing how the lower edge has worn away in a concave line.

Figure 16
Inside of a drawer front showing that there have been at least three sets of pulls. The present reproduction pull bolts are in the original holes, but there is another set of holes that held an intermediate pull.

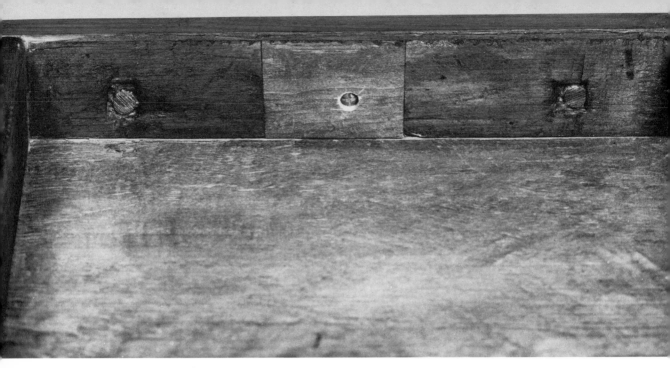

Figure 17 (above)
The inside of a drawer front from a late "Sheraton" bedside table. The holes for the two original pulls have been plugged. The head of the bolt for the present pull appears in the filled-in lock mortise. A strip of new wood covers the top of the drawer front and conceals the top of the lock mortise.

Figure 18
The outside of the front of the same drawer. There is no evidence of the original pull holes or of a keyhole. Taken with other evidence this clearly proves that the original front has been covered with a new piece of wood.

ways of one piece of wood with the grain usually running the longer dimension except in very small drawers. Because the sides of the drawers are relatively thin the grooves are comparatively shallow, and one will often find that the bottom has pulled completely out of one of the long-side grooves. Again, if the bottom has been nailed or glued in place, it will be split. Since drawers are normally constructed of softer woods, this shrinkage and its effects are usually very obvious. An additional effect of shrinkage in case pieces with drawers results from the fact that the side of the drawers are made with the grain running the long way while the exterior ends of the case itself are normally made with the grain running vertically. Thus the front-to-back shrinkage is greater in the case than in the drawer sides. If the drawers originally extended to the back of the piece, they will no longer go in all the way. This is the reason the drawers on many old case pieces protrude slightly. Or, if the owner has insisted on shoving them in forcefully, the back of the piece will be knocked loose. If none of these conditions appear in a case piece, look to make sure that no one has recently performed cosmetic surgery by shortening the drawers or by removing the stops that were often included when drawers were originally made slightly shallower than the case. If there is no trace of any of these developments, be very suspicious. The least that can have happened is that new drawers have been made for the original fronts.

Another feature which affords good evidence of age through shrinkage is the wooden pin which early cabinet makers often used to fasten different elements of their furniture together. These pins were almost invariably made of hard wood with the grain along their long axis. Thus shrinkage in length would be so little as to be almost nil. When these pins were put in place they were driven flush with the surface, but their relative stability over the years, contrasted with the shrinkage normally encountered in the elements which they joined, causes them to protrude in an antique piece. Sometimes they stick out almost as much as a sixteenth of an inch. The same thing is noticeable, though to a lesser degree, in the legs that pass all the way through the plank seat of a chair. You should be able at least to feel a slight protuberance even if you cannot see it distinctly.

DRAWERS

Drawers offer a wealth of other information, besides the clues left by shrinkage, about the authenticity of a case piece. Since they are normally of soft wood and have probably been opened and closed thousands of times there should be signs of wear on the bottoms of the runners and on the guides. First they become smooth from the continued friction. A rough surface on the bottom of a runner is an immediate cause of suspicion. Then they start to wear away. A drawer that is pulled out will come straight for a little way, then start to tip down to a greater or lesser degree depending upon the tightness of the fit and the weight of its contents. Thus the bottom of the runner will wear away in a concave line, and the tops of the back corners in many instances will begin to show wear. Sometimes drawers have worn so much that they have had to be repaired with a "half sole." But an old drawer that has seen any amount of use should show either a noticeable amount of wear or an obvious repair. Sometimes also you may find a scratch, often quite deep, along the outside of a drawer side. If there is such a scratch, the drawer should be pulled out and the inside of the case checked to see if there is a nail end or other projection that would have caused the scar. If there is no sign of any such projection ever having been there, it raises the suspicion that the drawer came from another piece of furniture or that that side of the drawer at least is a replacement. I have, it is true, occasionally seen inexplicable scratches on drawer sides where there was no question of authenticity, but they should always make you stop and think.

Drawer fronts, too, offer much evidence about originality and

Figure 19 (above)
An original "Sheraton" or "Hepplewhite" brass with one of its bolts and nut. Note carefully the shape of the bolt shank and the threads.

Figure 20
An original early 19th century drawer pull (*left*) and a modern reproduction of the same style (*right*). Again, compare the shanks and threads.

authenticity. If there is a lock or a mortise indicating that there was a lock at any time, you should check the bottom of the rail immediately above to see if there is a mortise for the bolt of the lock to enter. If there is no such mortise, it is a good assumption that the drawer or at least the drawer front does not belong. Over the years most drawers have had their pulls or handles replaced at least one or two times. Sometimes the original ones broke and had to be replaced or the owners sought to modernize their furniture by adding hardware of the current style. Unfortunately a good many of the changes have been made by modern dealers to "improve" the looks of a piece. Wooden or glass knobs of the early 19th century seem to have little appeal to the buying public today, and so many a drawer has been vandalized by having such knobs replaced by Chippendale or Sheraton brasses that are completely out of keeping. Such alterations are readily detectable on the basis of style, or by the presence of extra holes, usually more or less skillfully plugged, visible on the inside or sometimes even on the outside. In some cases if the piece has not been heavily re-finished, you can detect the outlines of the original hardware. If there are no extra holes or other signs of changes in hardware, you either have a real treasure with its original brasses—or with hardware that miraculously fit the original holes exactly—or a new drawer front.

If the brasses fit the scar marks in the wood underneath them exactly and if there is only one set of holes which have not been reshaped even a tiny bit to take posts that were either slightly wider or slightly closer together than those for which the holes were drilled, look carefully at the brasses themselves. Make sure they are the proper style for the piece of furniture, then check the backs to see if they are well patinated. If they are of a very early style, they should be attached by nails or cotter pins. If they are in the Chippendale style, make sure they are cast and not stamped from a sheet. The posts, too, should be cast, square or chamfered in section, with handcut threads that do not match modern stand-

Figure 21 (above left)
Front of a windsor chair (*upside down*) showing wear on the front of the foot and scars in the paint. Note also the scribed line to indicate the center of the stretcher.

Figure 22 (above right)
The back of the finial of an early 19th century painted chair showing wear from being tilted back against a wall.

Figure 23
Nineteenth century stool showing considerable wear on the foot-height stretchers.

Figure 24 (above)
Drawer front of an 18th century pipebox. Note how long use has worn the paint off the knob and around the base of the knob. This box has had two coats of paint in its history, and both have worn.

Figure 25
Portion of the lower door of a painted corner cupboard. Note the wear on the door and frame at the upper left corner. The present knob is a replacement. A scar on the frame just to the left of it indicates that there was once a pivoted latch. This is why the door was opened by grasping the upper left corner.

ards, and the nuts relatively thin with the threads tapped by hand to match those on the bolts. Sheraton and Hepplewhite and later brasses were customarily stamped from sheet brass, but their posts were cast and the threads cut by hand. Modern posts are uniformly machined and therefore round in section with standard threads. Mid-Victorian brasses may legitimately boast machined posts but they would be the first.

WEAR

Any piece of wood that has been used frequently will show signs of wear and usually scars from misuse or accidents. The amount of such evidence will depend on the hardness of the wood, the type of use it has had, and the length of time it has been in service. Soft wood will wear and scar more easily than hard wood. Parlor pieces from a wealthy and childless household will remain more perfect than kitchen or dining room furniture used by a large family or the customers of a country inn. The wear on drawer runners has already been mentioned, but there are many other obvious places to look. The feet of chairs that have been dragged across floors will bear evidence of the resultant abrasion. If the chair was seized by the top rail of the back so that it was dragged at an angle, either the front edges of the front feet or the rear edges of the back feet will be rounded off. Tilting the chair back will also cause similar rounding on the back corners of the rear feet. And if the chair has been tilted back against a wall frequently, there will be corresponding wear on the backs of the finials of the uprights of banister-back or slat-back chairs, the crest rails of more sophisticated chairs or the center of the bow of a windsor back. Front stretchers on chairs that are placed at a convenient height for a sitter's feet will show wear, often very heavy wear. The ends of the arms of chairs where they would be grasped by the hand will often be polished smooth and the finish worn away. Side chairs that have been pushed up tight against tables will bear dents made by the edge of the table top. Often this dent is so slight that it cannot be seen except under special lighting conditions, but it can almost always be felt if you run your hand down the face of the uprights. Tavern tables and other types with stretchers will show foot wear like that found on the front stretchers of chairs. The edges and corners of table tops will be rounded. There will be nicks from fingernails and other signs of wear and soil around door knobs, drawer pulls and frequently on the top free corner of a cupboard door, especially if it does not have a knob or other pull. And then there are the countless nicks, scratches and dents caused by accidents. Often these will be found on the underside of stretchers or the skirts of chests or desks where broom or mop handle have struck them as the housewife cleaned beneath.

These are just some of the more obvious signs of wear and use. Any place where contact has been made regularly will show some evidence of it, but you should make certain that there is a logical explanation for each bit of such evidence that you find. Wear and scars in illogical places are a sure warning of fakery. For instance, stretcher wear from feet will occur only in the places where a sitter would normally put his feet. It would be awkward if not impossible to jam one's feet tightly against the legs, and so the rounding should stop short of the ends of the stretchers. Also the outside upper edge of the stretcher should be worn far more heavily than the inside edge—and the lower inside edge should not be worn at all. Even a nick or dent in that area would be a rarity, though not a complete impossibility. I well remember examining a set of Hepplewhite shield-back chairs that the National Park Service inherited when it assumed responsibility for Arlington House in the early 1930's. They were a beautifully made set, but they showed wear and nicks in the most unlikely places, including the upper inside corners of the legs. If one or two chairs had a nick in such a location, one could overlook it as the result of a freak accident. But when almost every leg of every chair had these scars, it defied logic. And then when we noticed that the

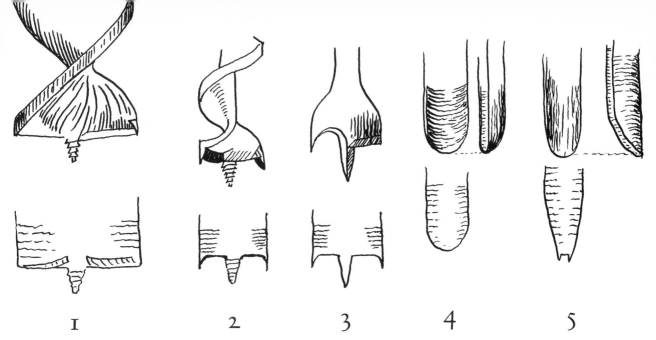

| 1 | 2 | 3 | 4 | 5 |

Figure 33
Some typical bits and cross sections of the holes they make. (1) a blacksmith-made hand auger of the early 19th century; (2) modern center shank bit; (3) 19th century center bit used mainly for shallow holes; (4) early spoon bit; (5) spoon bit variant. For both numbers (4) and (5) it is necessary to start the hole with a knife, but once started they are remarkably fast and efficient. *Courtesy Per E. Guldbeck.*

Figure 34 (*right*)
Score marks on the bottom of a windsor chair placed by the maker to help him locate the legs properly.

Figure 35 (*below*)
Some typical nails. (A) forged "rose head" nail; (B) forged nail with spatulate or chisel point; (C) brad with hand formed head; (D) forged "L"-head finish nail; (E) cut nail with forged head; (F) machine cut nail c. 1805 (after 1810 the points were usually cut square rather than beveled in one direction); (G) modern wire nail.

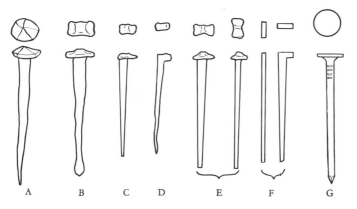

| A | B | C | D | E | F | G |

front corners of the rear feet were rounded as if from wear, we became even more suspicious. We could imagine no possible way in which such wear could have occurred in normal use to a complete set of chairs. The whole setup began to smell very strongly of fakery.

PATINATION

Almost as soon as wood is exposed to light and air, it begins to change color. This is especially true of unfinished wood, although stains and paint will also fade or discolor to some degree. Different woods discolor differently, even under identical conditions, but generally speaking identical woods that have been exposed to the same conditions will color identically. If they have not done so, something is wrong, and it usually signifies a replacement of some sort. This patination is usually most noticeable on the unfinished surfaces, such as a drawer sides and bottoms, the backs of case furniture or the underside of a tabletop.

Various parts of a piece of furniture are more exposed to light and air than other areas, and so there will be differences in patination even if all the parts are made of the same wood. The outside of the back of a case piece will usually be the most darkly patinated. The outside backs and sides of main drawers and the insides of cupboards will be slightly lighter. The little drawers behind the lid of a slant-top desk will be the least patinated of all because they have been most protected. But the whole back of the piece should be the same color if it is made of the same wood and the whole length and top edge of each drawer side should be the same. This combination of uniformity and variation because of degree of exposure is almost impossible to fake. Students have long noted that unfinished surfaces on English furniture tend toward blacks and grays while American woods are more yellow and brown. This is partly the result of the use of different secondary woods, but some students have also advanced the theory that English furniture has been more subjected to coal smoke than has American furniture where wood remained the standard fuel for open fireplaces for a much longer period. I have never been completely sold on this theory, myself, and no one seems to have taken into account the yellowing effects of tobacco smoke which has been so prevalent for the past three centuries or more—to say nothing of the sulphur and other industrial pollutants that have recently added their contributions to patination. Whatever the causes, it still remains true that similar woods that have been similarly exposed for an identical length of time will show an identical color. Be very wary of any variations that you cannot logically explain!

There are other kinds of patination and wear aside from the oxidation caused by exposure to light and air, smoke, etc. Dirt and grease from handling will also appear on frequently grasped areas, such as the underside of tabletops close to the edge, the area around the base of knobs on doors and drawers, the ends of chair arms, the upper edges of cabinet doors, and the like. Dealers usually try to clean this dirt off with solvents or damp cloths before offering a piece for sale, but if you can find an old specimen before it has had this cosmetic treatment, the dirt and grease stains are a comforting sign of age and use. Desk tops are frequently stained with ink and scratched from the pressure of pencil points. Kitchen table tops sometimes exhibit burns caused by a careless person setting a hot pan or kettle on them. Tool handles and gunstocks will be polished smooth and frequently discolored in the areas where they were most frequently grasped. It is a good idea to ask yourself where you would grasp any much-handled type of wooden artifact, and then look to see if there are any visible traces that others have left there in years gone by. Even objects not made of wood will often retain evidence of frequent grasping. I have felt thumb prints on the left side of the brim of an 18th century cocked hat where a left-handed wearer seized it to take it off or to tip it to an acquaintance. Even metals wear and patinate from such frequent handling in one customary spot.

TOOL MARKS

Despite conscientious smoothing with pumice or sandpaper plus years of wear, most wooden objects retain some traces left by the tools used by the original maker. They are most noticeable, of course, on the areas which would not normally be seen and so were never smoothed or sanded. These would include the backs, inside and out, of case pieces, the underside of drawer bottoms, the insides of seat rails on chairs and sofas, and so on. On completely unfinished wood, the most obvious marks are those left by the saw used to cut the wood. Hand saws leave straight lines from each cut, but they are not exactly parallel or precisely spaced and they are seldom perpendicular to the edge. Usually they slant. Lumber cut in a saw mill with a vertical blade will also exhibit straight lines, but they will be parallel, much more uniform in spacing and usually perpendicular. Either of these types of saw marks would be acceptable on early specimens—as would the uneven surface produced when a piece of wood was split instead of sawed. The radial lines left by a circular saw, however, are an entirely different matter. The circular saw appeared late in the 18th century, but it took many years for it to come into common use except for cutting veneer. It should be accepted only in Mid-Victorian or later pieces.

Next to saw marks, the most distinctive evidence from tools is probably that left by the "jointer" plane used for quick smoothing. Early plane blades usually had convex edges, and on roughly finished areas, such as the backs of case pieces or the undersides of drawers, one can often see a series of shallow broad grooves left by individual plane strokes. Even on highly finished areas the student with sensitive fingers can sometimes feel the faint rem-

Figure 26 (above left)
Supposed 18th century gun rack from Connecticut.

Figure 27 (above right)
Detail of the gun rack (the middle cross piece) disassembled. The hand forged nail is old and rusty, but there was no rust in the hole. The original paint is patinated and crackled. The paint on the new surfaces cut out to receive the gun barrels, on the other hand, is smooth.

Figure 28
The bottom of the gun rack shows the bottom boards patinated much more darkly than the side member. If they had always been together, they would have patinated the same since they are the same kind of wood and would have had the same exposure to light and air. Finally, the edge of the cut at the end of the bottom boards shows the "feathers" produced by a relatively recent cut of old wood.

Figure 29 (right)
Marks on a shingle split with a frow.
Courtesy Per E. Guldbeck.

Figure 30
Marks on the bottom of a drawer showing
it was cut by a hand-held frame saw. In
this case the cabinetmaker's saw was not
large enough for the job so he had to cut
from four different directions—and make
the cuts meet!

nants of such strokes. In either case these strokes should almost always run with the grain. Normally such plane marks are found only on pieces made before 1800 or by a country craftsman in a later era. Tiny, almost undetectable ripples running across the grain strongly suggest the use of a mechanical planer and therefore, modern work. The horizontal, parallel scratches left in concave areas are usually the marks of a drum sander and so again a warning of recent activity. If the scratches on a curved surface are vertical and uniformly spaced as well as parallel they quite probably indicate a power driven bandsaw, which is just as discouraging.

The holes drilled in chair uprights to receive the stretchers can also offer good evidence of age. The pod augers used for this purpose until the middle of the last century had a rounded point, and so the holes that they made terminate in a rounded end. The modern gimlet-point drill produces a hole with a flat end and a small cone-shaped extension in the center. This applies only to large holes. Small bits which left holes with a flat bottom and a pointed indentation in the center, very like those from modern bits, came into use in the 18th century.

Early furniture makers also frequently used score marks as guides which they often failed to sand off. One place where such marks can normally be detected is the side of a drawer where the maker scored a line to mark the limit of his cuts for dovetailing. Another frequent place for him to leave a score line is on a turned chair or table leg to indicate where it was to be drilled for a stretcher. Country or backwoods makers still use such score marks so they are not automatically a sign of age, but their presence is one more bit of corroborative evidence for hand craftsmanship.

Aside from the score marks there is one other evidence of hand workmanship in the dovetailing of a drawer or chest. Machine-cut dovetails produce tails and pins of identical dimensions. In handcut dovetails they should vary. It is an axiom in the antique field that dovetails of earlier pieces tend to be larger and fewer in number and therefore the narrower more numerous dovetails are indicative of later craftsmanship. Like all generalities, there are exceptions to this rule, but primarily it holds true.

FASTENERS

Fasteners such as nails, tacks and screws can be an excellent general sign of age but almost never a precise guide in dating a specimen. Nails have been in use for centuries—and on a much broader scale than often thought. The site of the 17th century English colony at Jamestown produced thousands of nails during excavations that are still only partially complete. And this was a time when, according to history, nails were so scarce they were carefully saved and reused. The archeological evidence certainly does not bear this out. Furniture makers of the 17th century used nails for attaching hinges, fastening fronts to drawers and dozens of other tasks that were later performed by screws. And they used brass tacks for upholstery. These early nails were hand forged from rod. The roughly rectangular shanks taper to either a sharp or spatulate point, and one can usually see irregularities from hammer marks along the sides. Heads might be large and formed by four hammer strokes into the so-called "rose head" or they might be rectangular and flat—or there might be no head at all.

Cut nails came into use at the very end of the 18th century. These nails were stamped from a sheet. They are rectangular in section and of a much more uniform taper with flat regular sides except for the burrs caused by the cutter. The taper is on one or two sides only. The other two opposing sides are parallel, and the "grain" runs crosswise. The earliest cut nails from about 1790–1810 have handmade heads. After that the heads are machine made. Wire nails with a flat round head, round shank and sharp cut points came into use after 1850.*

* The best study of nail design is Lee H. Nelson's, *Nail Chronology, Tech-*

Figure 31 (above left)
Marks made by a circular saw. *Courtesy Per E. Guldbeck.*

Figure 32 (above right)
The concave marks left by a "joiner" plane. *Courtesy Per E. Guldbeck.*

Figure 36
A selection of handmade screws from the 18th and 19th centuries. The most recent screw is second from the left. It comes from a model 1841 "Mississippi" rifle.

The difficulty in dating a piece closely by the type of nails used lies in the fact that isolated workmen continued to use hand-forged nails for many years after the cut variety appeared. Also older pieces were sometimes taken apart and renailed with more modern types. In these cases, however, one can usually find traces of the holes made by the original fasteners. Even if the same holes are used it is sometimes possible to detect the fact that the present nail is not the first to have been driven in. Fakers are not necessarily obtuse when it comes to using nails either, and they will often save and use old nails in their forgeries. I recall well an "18th century gun rack" offered to the National Park Service complete with a provenance stating that it came from an inn used as a militia muster point in Connecticut. It was indeed made of old wood in a good period design, but the shelf on which the butts of the muskets would have rested bore absolutely no dents or scars such as would normally have resulted from a group of men in various degrees of sobriety racking up their muskets. The fasteners were all handmade nails of the proper type for the period, but when a few were carefully extracted they were found to be covered with rust. Yet there were no traces of rust stains in the nail holes which should have been there if the nails had rusted in situ. The only possible conclusion was that the maker had used old rusted nails when he put the rack together. Conceivably an 18th century craftsman might have reused some old nails when he made such a piece, but this negative evidence combined with the lack of dents or scars in logical places led to an even closer examination that turned up marks from both a bandsaw and a drum sander. As a sort of anticlimax the Park Service ended up purchasing the rack since none of us had ever seen an original specimen for sale and this one was cheaper than having a reproduction made in our own shops. But at least we knew we were not

nical Leaflet 48, published by the American Association for State and Local History, Nashville, Tenn., 1968.

buying an original—and we did not pay the price an original should have commanded.

Like nails, screws have passed through several evolutionary stages. The earliest wood screws that one is apt to encounter in furniture or gunstocks date from the late 17th century, and for many years thereafter they were used far less frequently than nails. These early wood screws were forged and had their threads cut by hand. They are frequently slightly irregular in shape, and the points are blunt if not actually cut off square. The heads may be slightly out of round, and the slots are narrow and sometimes off center. To use such a screw the craftsman had first to drill a hole the full length of his screw though of a slightly smaller diameter and then turn the screw in with considerable force. If you take a screw out of an old piece of furniture, you will note that it will not hold nearly as well when you replace it. Also you are apt to find that similar-looking screws from the same piece must be put back in their original holes since there are tiny dimensional differences that usually keep them from being interchangeable.

Making screws by hand was a time-consuming operation, and so their use continued to be restricted for many years. On gunstocks screws did not replace nails for attaching buttplates until about 1720. In furniture screws first seem to have come into use for attaching hinges, then for attaching tabletops to their frames, fastening cleats to the underside of chest lids or tabletops and for securing locks. It was 1750 before screws became really common and were used for many purposes. Between 1789 and 1834 a host of inventors in England and America developed screw-making machinery, and then their use really proliferated. Their appearance also changed. Points remained blunt, but the shanks became truly round. The gimlet point so familiar on modern screws was designed in France as early as the mid-18th century, but it did not come into general use until after 1850. One unfortunate fact about screws, however, is that it is far more difficult to detect when a modern screw found in a supposed antique is merely a replacement for an earlier type than is the case with a nail. The cutting action of the threads changes the hole so radically that all evidence of an earlier fastener is usually completely destroyed. A few modern screws in a piece are therefore not necessarily evidence of recent manufacture, but the presence of a complete set of period screws is a great comfort, especially if the slots in their heads do not show evidence of recent use.

Another sort of fastener, though in quite a different category from the nail and the screw, is the smooth-turned dowel as opposed to the peg which was normally not completely round in section. The dowelled joint so familiar in modern cabinet work is a relatively recent development which first came into use about the middle of the last century. You will frequently find a dowel joint in an older piece of furniture, but it will be the work of a modern restorer seeking to strengthen a loosened joint that was originally weak or to repair a break. Such use should cause no alarm. But a chair in the Chippendale style with originally dowelled joints will suggest a reproduction made for the Centennial of U. S. Independence in 1876 or even later.

EMBELLISHMENTS, MARRIAGES AND DIVORCES

The most frequent kinds of fakes that the collector or curator encounters in furniture are pieces that have been "improved" through the addition of carving or inlaying, combining elements of different origin to form a more important piece or altering a surviving fragment of one type of furniture so that it appears to be something entirely different. In collector jargon, the assembled piece from two or more originals is known as a "married piece" or a hybrid. The reworking of a single element into a seemingly complete object is called a "divorced" piece or an "orphan."

Figure 37 (above)
"Seventeenth century" chest assembled from various elements in the Victorian era. The carving along the top and the center marquetry panel date about 1850. The outer marquetry panels are 17th century as are the other carved elements, but they come from several different chests.

Figure 38
Details of one of the 17th century marquetry panels. The fact that it does not belong in its present position is immediately evident because the base of the vase in the design has been covered over. The supporting figures have been carved by a different hand than the arch above them, and they do not quite fit. They obviously do not belong together.

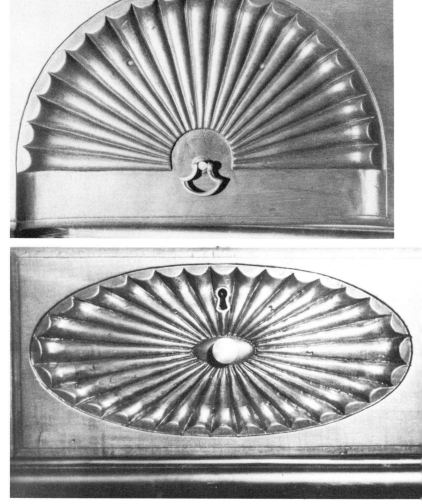

Figures 39 A & B (right)
Two carved designs from a "married" highboy. The shell carving from the lower portion is original, done by a skilled carver. The oval carving was added to an upper drawer to help tie the two pieces together. The carving is less skillful and sure, and the keyhole is intrusive.

Figure 40 (below)
Cross-sections of the knees of two carbiole legs. The section on the left is of a leg intended originally for decoration, and the carving juts out beyond the normal curve of the knee. The leg at right was embellished later. The carving is shallow and remains within the original curve of the knee.

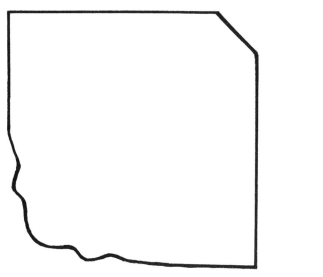

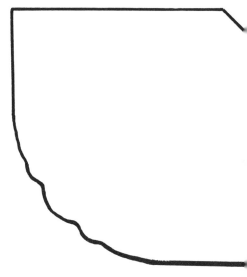

Figure 41 (above left)
Although this English jewel chest is not a married piece, it shows some of the signs of different workmanship and materials that one should look for in assessing a married piece.

Figure 42 (above right)
A selection of the drawers from the chest in the preceding illustration. Note that the upper drawer has a poplar side while the lower drawers have oak sides. Also there are three distinctly different styles of dovetailing. These drawers were evidently made by different workmen at different times. Probably none is original to the piece.

Figure 43 (below left)
This "table" is a good example of a divorced piece. Originally it was the lower section of a 17th century English cupboard. The boards on both the top and the shelf are old but taken from a building or some other piece. The height, style and proportion are wrong for a table.

Figure 44 (below right)
Detail of the "table" in the previous illustration. The fact that only two of the legs are decorated indicates that the piece was originally intended to stand against a wall.

Normally it is relatively easy to recognize one of these fakes if one knows where to look.

The most difficult fakes to determine are those that have been embellished by adding carving or inlay. This work attempts to convert a piece that was originally a simple object into a more elaborate and therefore a more desirable and more expensive piece. In the case of either carving or inlay one looks first to see if the style and workmanship is of the period of the object it graces and if it is well done. Not all carvers of past centuries were great artists, but normally they did know what they were doing from years of apprenticeship. Old carving is thus usually sure handed and not tentative or indecisive. And all carving or inlay on a piece should reflect the same workmanship and technique. In my own collection is a chest which violates every one of these tenets (Figure 37). It has some good 17th century marquetry inlay and some original 17th century carving. But it also has some Victorian carving, which is much better than the early carving, and some Victorian marquetry, which is not nearly as good as the 17th century marquetry. All of these elements have been combined in a frame of about 1850 following in general a style of about 1600 but with fretwork on the feet brackets that is purely Victorian. Obviously it is a chest that was constructed during the revived interest in the Elizabethan era that swept Britain and America in the mid-19th century. It was indeed a fake in its day, but now it has acquired at least some dignity as a genuine antique of the Elizabethan or Jacobean Revival.

When a modern carver goes to work on an old piece of wood he exposes unfinished surfaces that have not previously been open to light and air and thus have not patinated. He has to try to color these areas of new wood so that they blend with the untouched surface. He may use stain or dirt or a combination of both, but normally this is quite obvious. More often he ends up refinishing the whole piece. Thus a refinished antique with carving that is even slightly questionable is a piece to be regarded with considerable suspicion—and usually to be left unpurchased.

An additional bit of evidence to look for in assessing whether an inlay or carved decoration is original is sometimes offered by scratches and dents. If a surface scratch runs right up to the edge of an inlaid decoration, then disappears and picks up again on the other side of the inlay, obviously the inlay was added after the scratch was made—and that would have been highly unlikely on a surface that was decorated when it was new. The maker would have smoothed out all scratches before he did the inlay. Similarly a sharp object scratching the surface of a drawer face or the fall board of a desk with a carved ornament will have an effect on the carving as well. The type of effect will depend upon the nature of the object doing the scratching and also on the nature of the carving—whether relief or intaglio. Whatever the appearance of the scar is, you should always look at it carefully and see if it can be logically explained.

When a cabinet maker constructed a piece intended for embellishment with relief carving, he left extra wood for that purpose. A tilt-top table designed to have a raised "pie crust" edge would have an extra thick top so that the center portion could be cut away, leaving the raised edge. When the modern "embellisher" seeks to convert a plain tabletop into one with a raised and carved border he normally finds that the wood is not thick enough for him to cut away the center. Thus he will usually glue the carved border on the original surface. An applied border or any other carved decoration that has been applied to the surface of an antique before the Victorian period is thus an immediate danger signal. When no extra wood is added, new carving on an old piece will necessarily be shallow, and the highest areas will still fall within the general lines of the piece and not rise out from it. This is especially noticeable when new carving has been added to the knees of cabriole legs or to the columnar supports of pedestal stands or tables.

Marriages usually involve adding a bookcase or cabinet top to a simple slant-top desk to make it into a secretary bookcase or placing an old highboy top on a chest of drawers to make it into a chest on chest or some similar combination intended to utilize odd parts. This sort of marriage is very common in the antique trade despite the fact that it is almost impossible to manage it skillfully enough to fool anyone with a half-trained eye. First of all the styles and sizes must blend perfectly or you can spot the deception easily. If the top is slightly narrower and thinner than its newly found base, it is sometimes possible to conceal the mis-mating with a heavy molding, but still the piece will usually look out of balance if the two pieces do not belong together. If the upper piece is deeper than the base so that it protrudes even as little as half an inch at the back, it is a sure sign that something is wrong. Normally these large pieces were designed so that the upper and lower elements could be taken apart easily for convenience in moving—and this is one reason why they have frequently become separated. Thus it is always a good idea to lift the upper section slightly—just enough to see if the top of the lower portion has been finished. If it has, it is a sign that it was intended to be seen and so probably did not have another section on top of it when it was made.

There are other even more obvious signs to look for in detecting a marriage. For one thing the back of both the upper and lower sections of a true specimen should have patinated identically. If they are of two different colors, they have not always been together. A cabinet maker normally used the same secondary woods for any piece he was making. Thus if he used pine and poplar in the base, in nine cases out of ten he would have used pine and poplar in the upper portion also. Certainly he wouldn't have made such a radical change as to use oak and ash. Also, his workmanship would be the same. The dovetailing would be the same and so would the other techniques of drawer construction. Any variation in woods or workmanship is a warning. Perhaps there has been a repair or one drawer has been replaced—or maybe you have a married piece. Think it over carefully.

Another frequent anomaly in the antique trade is the divorced piece. An unscrupulous dealer may find himself with the base of a highboy and decide to convert it into a lowboy. Or he may have just the top of a highboy or the upper chest of a chest on chest and decide to convert it into a simple chest or a chest on frame by building a new frame or a new base. In any case, the prospective buyer should check the top of the lowboy to see if it is old, looking for tool marks, wear and patination and making sure there are no signs of new cuts to convert an old top to new dimensions. Then he should look underneath at the joint between the top and the base to see how they are fastened together and if there are signs of alterations of any kind. For new bases, feet or frames, the wear or lack of it on the bottoms of the feet offer excellent evidence of age. So do tool marks and the usual scars that come with age and use.

In this regard it should be noted that new feet are not necessarily damning on an antique chair, table, chest or whatever. Feet took an especially heavy beating. Movement on floors caused hard wear in many instances. I have seen a number of 17th-century joint stools in which the feet have been worn down by more than half. Sometimes, when furniture became outdated, it was stored in a basement or outbuilding with dirt floors, and the feet suffered from rot and insect attack. Some chairs were shortened for the use of smaller people or converted to rockers or set on casters—all operations involving the removal of all or part of the feet. The replacement of feet on furniture that has suffered in one of these ways is, I think, a legitimate repair—but the buyer should be aware of it, and he should expect to make his purchase for a lower price than a comparable piece with original feet would command.

WORM HOLES

I suppose there are probably more myths about worm holes circulating among antique collectors than about any other phase of the subject. Actually these holes are caused by insects—powerpost beetles, death-watch beetles or, in some instances, termites. Beginning collectors often look upon such holes as a sure sign of age, but they are no such thing. They can occur at any time, in new furniture as well as old. The insects and their larvae which make the holes enter the wood, then turn and tunnel along the grain, or occasionally across it, but always beneath the surface. This behavior is a good guide in detecting true worm holes from false ones. Even more important, it indicates whether the holes were made after the piece was constructed or whether the object was made from a piece of wood that was already infested. If the infestation occurred after the object was made, only a series of slightly out-of-round holes should appear on the surface. If there are a series of channels along the surface, either the object was made from infested wood—which no self-respecting cabinet maker or gunstocker would have done—or else the piece was reworked or sanded down so heavily that the channels have been exposed. In either case it makes the piece undesirable. I remember once seeing in a shop a Baltimore cellarette that attracted me greatly. When I pulled it out from the wall, however, I noticed the channels from worm holes on the backs of two of the legs. Warned by this, I gave the piece a thorough inspection and found the feet innocent of wear and the bottoms of the drawer runners rough to the touch. The bellflower inlays were beautifully done, but the piece proved to be an original cellarette case with a brand new stand. Thus worm holes can indeed be important in determing the age of a piece, but purely in a negative sense.

One of the hoariest of tales about worm holes involves the faker who picks up his trusty shotgun and fires a load of birdshot at his finished piece to produce the effect of worm holes. This tale has been repeated so often that many people accept it as fact but it is sheer poppycock that can only be believed by someone who has never fired a shotgun at a piece of wood. For one thing, if the shooter stands close enough to get any penetration in a dense wood, he will be so close that one can see the pattern of the shot on

Figure 45 (right)
"Worm" channels in the top of a 17th century chest. In this case these channels are not a warning. The tops have merely broken through, leaving more than half the channel in the wood. If half or less remains in the wood, it is a sign that the piece has been sanded down heavily or made from a piece of wood that already had the channels in it, something no self-respecting cabinet maker would have done.

Figure 46 (center right)
Duck decoy of the early 20th century. *Courtesy Per E. Guldbeck.*

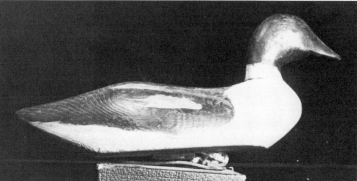

Figures 47 A & B (below) .
Bottom of the decoy in the previous illustration showing the various things that indicate its age: (1) areas of black paint underlying the present coat of white paint which itself shows signs of age; (2) slit for an earlier keel which has long since deteriorated though little fragments of rusted iron remain in the slit; (3) brass screw-eye, heavily patinated with a piece of cord in the eye that is tinted green from long contact with the brass; (4) a lead weight used to replace the earlier keel. The iron nails are heavily corroded from water and bi-metallic contact. The rust is not only on the nail heads but on the surrounding lead, indicating that they rusted in place. *Courtesy Per E. Guldbeck.*

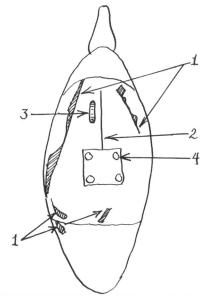

a flat surface. If he fired at an element that was not flat—a turned table leg for instance—some of the pellets would strike the sides and cut nicks and channels in a straight line across the grain. There is no way a load of birdshot can produce holes even remotely resembling those caused by insects.

I have seen worm holes made by drill bits, but these are easily detected because they are perfectly round and go straight in. True insect holes are neither truly round nor straight. Also the drilled holes will be the size of a standard bit. Actually the faker who wants worm holes can obtain real ones with very little effort. All he has to do is put his gunstock, his table leg or whatever in a pile of infested planks or logs in a basement or outbuilding, and in a couple of months or less he will have all the genuine holes he wants.

DECOYS

An area of collecting that has developed rapidly in recent years is that of wooden decoys used by wildfowl hunters. Most of the real ones that turn up on the market are fairly recent and so one cannot look for tool marks in the same way that he can on older objects. A perfectly genuine decoy may show striations from a circular saw or a bandsaw. There are some evidences of age and use, however, that can help to eliminate at least the poorer fakes. A decoy that has been used will show the effects of weather and water. The grain will be raised, and there should be little chips and slivers missing. Also a few scars from birdshot are a comforting sign. Usually there will be an old weight—a piece of lead or iron strap—or at least the holes from the fasteners of such a weight used to hold the decoy upright in the water. If the original paint has remained, it will be weathered—and it will be hard. Sun and water will cause it to crawl and crack and flake off in places. It will be so hard that you cannot nick it with your fingernail, but you can shatter and crack it with pressure from a blunt point.

Figure 48 (above)

A fine blanket chest of about 1700 that offers a good case study in things to look for in evaluating furniture. Originally the top of this chest lifted up, and the top two drawers were dummies. At some time during its history it was modified by fastening the top down and making the dummy drawers into real ones. The left front foot is a restoration; the right foot is original. Despite these alterations this is still a highly desirable piece of furniture because of its rarity, but a purchaser should have noted the details shown in the accompanying pictures.

Figure 49

Chest with drawers removed. Note the difference in patination on the pieces that have been added to make the upper two drawers functional.

Figure 50 (top)
The original right front foot. Note the wear on the bottom and the scars. The even patination on the bottom of the side boards shows that this chest always had separate front feet. (On many the side boards continued down as feet. Sometimes these were cut off and the more decorative ball feet added to enhance the value of the piece, but not on this one.) The damage on the corners is a good sign of age and use and would not disturb a serious collector.

Figure 51
The replaced left front foot. Compare the finish and lack of scars with the appearance of the original foot in the previous illustration. Note also the line around the base of the foot showing the area covered by the original foot on this side.

Figure 52 (above)
Detail of the back showing nails with large hand forged heads and a rust stained area around them proving that they rusted in place.

Figure 53
Another area of the back showing the holes where the original cotterpin (staple) hinges were removed when the top was fixed down instead of opening as it had originally.

Also it should be an oil base paint, not an alkyd or acrylic or rubber base variety. All of these signs will be present if a decoy has been used for only twelve or fifteen years, and there is no way that I know of to determine whether a used decoy is fifteen or fifty years old—but at least you can often tell a genuine used decoy from one that was made only recently for selling to the completely gullible.

In the evaluation of any antique artifact made of wood, the best advice is to look at it from all points of view. Check the evidence of shrinkage, wear, weather, tool marks, workmanship and the rest in the context of the piece as a whole. Some pieces will measure up in all respects, and some you can reject outright. But there will be some in which most of the evidence seems good but you have doubts on one or two points. If you can think of no logical explanation of these apparent aberrations, you have to decide for yourself whether you can live with the item or not.

Be careful how hard you strain to find logical explanations for incongruities. In my personal experience I have often tended to err when I wanted an object badly. I have made excuses and bought a piece only to become convinced after living with it that my first instincts were right and I should have let it alone. As an example, some years ago I saw a fine fanback windsor in the shop of an honest dealer from whom I had purchased many good pieces over the years. It was just the chair I needed for my library, and the dealer felt it was perfectly good except for the fact that it had been refinished and all the original paint removed. I looked it over carefully, and it appeared to be correctly made and in perfect style. There was wear on the stretcher, perhaps a little too much wear, for the center swelling was absolutely flat on top. The thing that bothered me most was the fact that the legs did not protrude above the seat even slightly, and the pegs did not stick out either. I wanted the chair so badly that I decided that it could well have been that the refinisher had sanded down the tops of the chair legs and the ends of the pins so that they were flush. Still I had enough misgivings that I asked the dealer if I could take the piece home with me for one night to see how it "fit" in the place I intended to use it. Since I was an old customer he kindly agreed. The chair fit the place I had in mind beautifully, and I spent a good part of the evening looking at it and cogitating. Finally a light dawned. There was a scratch on the seat of the chair—which in itself was a good sign—but the scratch had shellac in it and it went right across the end of one of the legs where it came through the seat. If the leg had been sanded down during the refinishing as I had convinced myself it had, the scratch would have been completely eradicated from the leg end. Therefore the scratch had to have been made after the refinishing but before the shellacking. Stirred by this I got busy again and dug out my high intensity light. When I turned the chair upside down and applied the light in a raking manner it turned up incontrovertible evidence of a mechanical planer. The chair was a fine reproduction, perhaps fifty years old, but that was all. I returned the chair in the morning, and the dealer, who I am certain honestly believed the piece genuine, took it back without question.

This is a long story, but it illustrates my point. Look at every aspect of an antique piece before you reach a conclusion—and don't let your desire for it seduce you into making too many excuses for minor shortcomings.

3 | Metals

Metals offer the connoisseur almost as many signs of age as wood. Metals do not shrink with the passage of time as wood does, but even the hardest show marks from wear and scars from abuse. All those commonly encountered except gold and platinum also oxidize and patinate, and most objects made of metal bear evidence of the techniques of manufacture—as well as signs of alteration—if you are skilled enough to recognize them.

Of these clues, oxidation or patination is one of the first and most important signs that a trained curator or collector checks after he has assured himself that the piece is stylistically correct for type and period. It is possible that an iron or steel artifact that has always been kept in a dry place and protected with oil or wax will show no traces of rust, or that a bronze which was artificially patinated by the founder and stored under good conditions will still be found in pristine condition. But these are the exceptions rather than the rule. The chances are that at some time in the object's history at least a slight oxidation will have occurred, and even an ancient cleaning will leave blemishes, however slight, in the original finish. Likewise, artificially oxidized bronzes will often show wear on high spots or on their bottoms if they have been handled with any frequency.

One of the axioms you should always bear in mind about oxi-

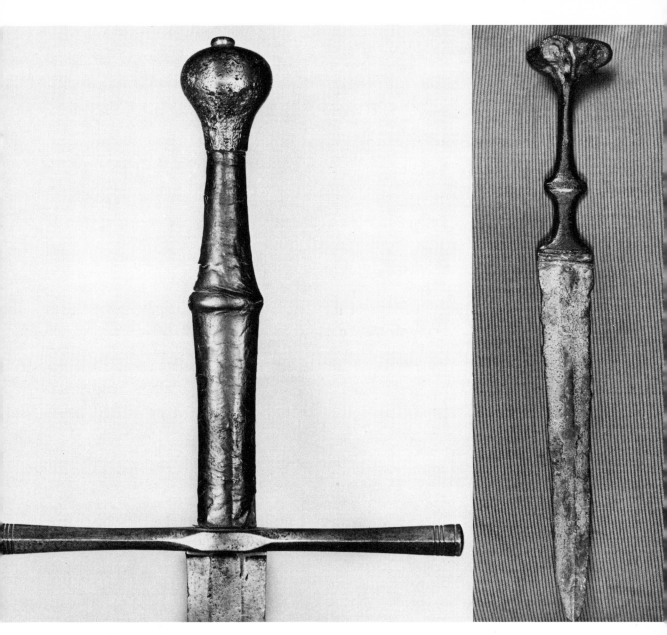

Figure 54 (above left)
The heavy pitting on the pommel of this sword is in sharp contrast to the lightly pitted crossguard and blade. Even if there were not stylistic differences the oxidation alone would indicate that this is an assembled piece.

Figure 55
The difference in the patination between the hilt and blade of this bronze dagger from Luristan indicated that they had not always been together. The discovery of a solder joint confirmed it.

dation is that an object made of two or more pieces of the same metal will normally patinate at the same rate and in the same pattern on all the exposed surfaces of each part. Finger prints from damp hands can cause isolated areas of rust on steel or iron, and keeping a knife or sword blade in a leather scabbard, which frequently holds moisture or residual acids from the tanning process, can cause these blades to rust more rapidly than the steel parts of the hilt. But always be sure that there is a good logical explanation for any differences in the amount or type of rusting. If there is none, the chances are that the piece has been assembled from parts and not originally made in its present form.

As mentioned before, collectors and curators alike are frequently their own worst enemies in evaluating such evidence. We often want a piece so badly that we start making excuses for the differences in color or the amount of pitting instead of rejecting the fraud outright. An example in my own experience is the bronze dagger from Luristan (Figure 55). Bronze pieces from that part of Iran are by no means uncommon on today's market, and this one had a perfectly good pedigree as far as it could be traced. It had been sent by a man in the diplomatic service to a relative as a gift. Seeing an exhibition of Luristan bronzes at a local arms show, the relative asked the collector at the table if such daggers had any value. The collector suggested a very modest sum, and the owner brought the piece in and sold it. Within a few days it was offered to me. With its sculptured rams' heads it was an exceptionally handsome example and a type that I did not have. The difference in color between the hilt and the blade (normally cast in one piece or with a hilt of the same alloy cast on) was instantly visible, and I should have rejected it just as instantly. But I desired such a dagger greatly, and I began trying to rationalize the difference. Salt and oils from long handling might have caused the hilt to turn a deeper green, I imagined—and I convinced myself despite my better judgment. It was not until several months later, while examining the hilt under bright light and magnification,

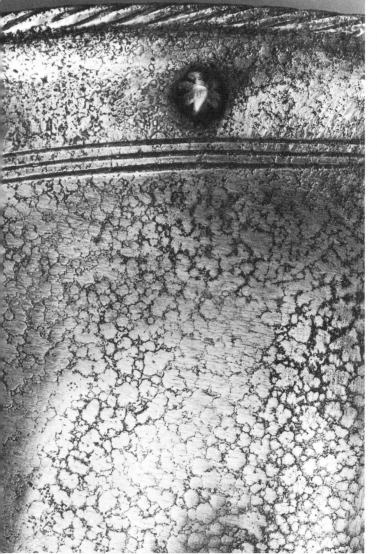

Figure 56 (above)
A signature recently inlaid in gold on an iron surface that had already pitted. Note how the gold has "flowed" out of line and into pits, especially on the upright lines of the "H" and the inner line of the "O". *Courtesy Stanley M. Diefenthal.*

Figure 57
Patination pattern produced on iron by the use of acid.

that I discovered faint traces of file marks on the pommel. The iron file had not been invented when this piece had supposedly been made. Again I tried to rationalize. Perhaps someone had tried to remove mineral deposits. But this would have caused a change in color in the filed area—and there were no differences, even in the depths of the file marks. Spurred on, I made further tests and finally found traces of a solder joint cleverly covered with paint and sand between the blade and hilt. What I had so happily clasped to my bosom these many months was actually an old blade to which someone had added a new hilt, cast from another dagger. It promptly moved from my bronze collection to my collection of fakes, and I had learned once again that the old axiom about similar oxidation is still true. It is a good thing to remember. It doesn't matter if the piece is a weapon, a candlestick or a pair of pipe tongs.

Oxidation offers other sorts of clues as well. Frequently a faker will try to enhance the value of a piece by adding the name of a well known maker. If the piece had originally been marked by a lesser craftsman, this involves polishing out the old mark. Sometimes it is done so skillfully that only a sensitive eye or finger can trace the depression resulting from this heresy, but the patination will always be disturbed—and usually quite visibly so. If an unmarked rusted iron object has had a name added either by stamping or engraving, the new lines will cut through the pitting. Look at the marks through a magnifying glass and see if this is the case. The new marks will also usually be smooth below the level of the pitting on the original surface. Old engraving will normally have pits in the vertical walls of the cuts and along the bottom. New cuts will be smooth even if the forger has thought to rub dirt or lampblack into the lines to hide clean surfaces. Old marks will also be soft and smooth to the touch. Hard, sharp edges are an immediate sign of new work. Only the least skilled fakers will leave these sharp edges, but when they polish them off, they again disturb the surface patina!

On fakes made from scratch, the forger will often try to produce a patina that resembles a natural one. On iron or steel he frequently employs an acid. This is usually detectable because it is so uniform. Real rusting normally develops patterns, however slight, of more and less pitted areas. Also it is sometimes possible to detect a distinct overall pattern on an acid-rusted surface where the acid has collected in droplets. Unlike normal moisture which produces rust slowly, acid acts swiftly and delineates the shapes of these drops.

The oxidation of soft metals such as silver, brass, bronze, copper or pewter is quite different from the rusting of iron or steel. Usually fakers produce a false patina quickly by using a form of sulphur. A piece of silver placed in a closed container with liver of sulphur or a similar product will develop a tarnish that is often impossible to distinguish from an old patination since in most cases it is the sulphur in the air that causes genuine tarnish. On copper, brass, or bronze, however, it produces a very ugly black color that is not at all natural in appearance. These metals usually develop a greenish or brown patination when it forms naturally. Black should raise instant suspicion. Another technique used on copper is to sprinkle copper sulphate on their surfaces and bake them in an oven. This compound forms a hard, glass-like green oxide that will break away if it is scraped by a sharp instrument. Also copper sulphate tends to draw up into beads when it melts, and so the patination is usually spotty and unnatural in appearance. The quickest and easiest method of imparting a spurious appearance of age is to rub a green powder, such as Paris Green, into the deep recesses in the surface. This can quickly be removed with a fingernail and should fool no one. But still the fakers use it now and then. Even paint or pigment in oil is sometimes used, but these, too, are easily detected—if you look closely and "feel" the patina with the point of a pin or knife. Real oxidation has to be scoured or scraped off. It adheres tightly to the surface. Paint will peel away or come off in curls. There are chemical techniques that produce very convincing patinas. Burial in manure for an extended period will also work. In such cases your only clues are the over-uniform color of the oxidation. This is not a very good clue, however, and for this reason you must look especially for correct style, signs of manufacturing techniques and wear.

MATERIALS AND
METHODS OF MANUFACTURE

If you are going to purchase any kind of metal artifacts you should be thoroughly familiar with how the objects you are interested in were made and the types of materials that were used to produce them. If an object has been made incorrectly—cast in a mold, perhaps, when it should have been die-struck or beaten out with a hammer—note the discrepancy and reject it immediately. This seems like a truism, yet fakes made improperly and from the wrong materials continually appear on the market and frequently fool the unwary.

One such badly made fake that I saw only recently showed almost every error possible in these categories. But this did not prevent the dealer who owned it—I hope innocently—from trying to feature it at one of the most prestigious antique shows in the United States. The purported antique was an iron candle stand with a tripod base and an arm holding two brass candle sockets. The vertical portion of the stand consisted of a modern machine-made iron rod with a scattering of odd nicks and dents in a naive attempt to suggest hand forging. The tripod base had been fashioned from rolled sheet iron and attached to the rod by a bolt instead of being riveted in the way an 18th-century craftsman would have done. The brass swirled finial at the top—which may have been old—had been riveted in place instead of screwing on in the usual fashion. The cross arm was made of rolled iron, and the brass candle sockets had been fastened on with modern carriage bolts. Even a half-trained or sleepy connoisseur could spot

Figure 58 (right)
Fake U. S. Marine Corps buckle of "unknown" pattern. The patina is typical of that produced by liver of sulphur. In addition to this and some problems with the engraving style, the maker stamped the motto "FORTITUDINE" which would never have been done—even if the letters had been in period style instead of modern. *Courtesy Robert H. McCauley.*

Figure 59
Reproduction of ancient Chinese bronze knife money. The "patina" is painted on and is singularly unconvincing. When imported, these reproductions along with many other forms bear a paper label that says "Made in Hong Kong". It is surprising how often these labels disappear.

this feeble fake from across the room, but it was offered to me for a sum well over a thousand dollars without even the trace of a blush.

Any handmade item will usually bear some marks that indicate the method of manufacture. Wrought iron or softer metals formed by hammering will show the marks of the hammer or the embossing tool. It is in this area that many fakers are led astray by their exuberance. Every hammer mark should have a purpose. The early smiths hammered only when necessary, and they kept their strokes as unobtrusive as possible. On the finished surfaces of fine work they removed them with a planishing hammer and then by filing or polishing. But the inner surfaces, not intended to be seen, usually retain the marks as do rough implements, hardware, and so on. These hammer marks are shallow and softly rounded dents or, on a convex surface, a series of small flats or facets. They never produce the pock-like overall pattern of small sharp dents that one finds in modern "old timey" hardware for the "Early American Home." Embossing tools usually leave a series of short straight lines or dents, depending upon the type of tool used. But these will be on the inner surface only.

Cast pieces of brass or pewter were often finished on a lathe if the shape lent itself to this treatment. The lathe marks were polished out of the visible surface, but if you look at the bottoms of candle sticks with circular bases or of Britannia ware plates made in the late 18th and most of the 19th century, you will normally see a series of concentric rings left by the lathe work. It was not until the stamping technique became common after 1850 that the lathe marks disappeared. These marks of the finishing lathe should not be confused with the somewhat similar series of concentric rings found all over the outer surfaces of one-piece brass or copper kettles and bed warmers. These are signs that the piece was made by "spinning," a technique that did not become popular for brass objects until after 1850, and therefore a sign of late manufacture. Early copper and brass kettles were made of two or

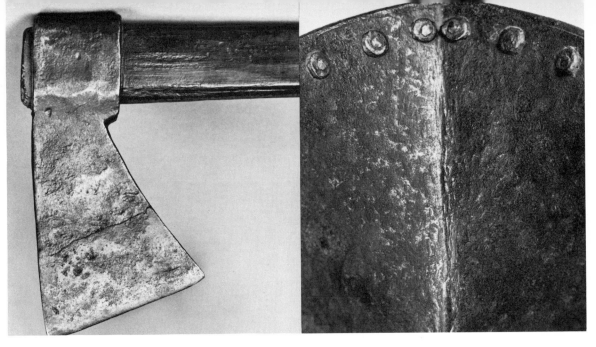

Figure 60 (above left)
Roughly forged hatchet of the late 18th century. Note that the hammer marks are soft and appear only where necessary.

Figure 61 (above right)
The inside of an early 16th century bevor (guard for the lower face). Since this surface was not meant to be seen the hammer marks have been left, as have the short straight lines made by the tool used to form the ridge on the center of the outer surface. Note also the good uniform patination, especially around the undisturbed rivet heads.

Figure 62 (below left)
Top view of an early copper still. This still was hammered out and the top fastened on with brazed dovetail joins visible here as the lighter colored lines and areas in a generally circular pattern level with the handle rivets. In this instance the top has been made in two pieces so there is a second diagonal joint in line with the right handle rivet. *Photo by John Diehl.*

Figure 63
Inside bottom of an early hammered copper kettle showing a tight dovetail joint around the edge and no sign of turning or spinning. *Photo by John Diehl.*

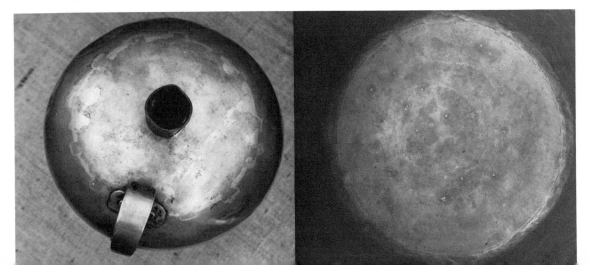

Figure 64 (above)
Pewter spoon newly cast in an original early 18th century mold. It has not been trimmed and so the sprue can be seen at the tip of the bowl and the flashing where the metal seeped out between the two halves of the mold can be seen along the handle and especially at the tip.

Figure 65 (below left)
Base of an 18th century bronze grinding mortar showing the wear and scratches that one would expect after years of use and storage.

Figure 66
Base of an early 19th century bronze grinding mortar. This one was slightly turned to smooth it after casting as shown by the concentric rings. Still the center and rim are slightly higher and so are burnished from continuous contact with the table top.

three pieces, soldered or brazed together, or else they were made of a single sheet hammered or "raised" over a stake. Britannia, a metal resembling pewter but tougher and brighter, lent itself more easily to the spinning technique than brass or copper. Thus manufacturers were spinning Britannia at least as early as 1825.

A cast specimen that should have been wrought or struck can usually be identified quickly. Often the cast piece will be slightly thicker than one that has been wrought and considerably thicker than die-struck objects, such as some belt plates, hat plates or buttons. Occasionally a careless faker will leave traces of the seams where the mold separated. These show up as very faint ridges. Any faker worth his salt will file these off, but sometimes there are areas where it is difficult to do this—around the edges of a milled coin, for instance, or in the depressions of a relief ornament. These mold lines occur only when solid two-piece or multiple-piece molds are used. An investment casting leaves no such traces, but there is still the spot where the sprue from the pouring inlet has to be cut off. Sometimes signs of this can be found. If not, you have to look for other evidence. Some detail is always lost when a copy is cast in a mold made from an original piece. The small lines and the edges of raised ornaments will not be quite as crisp as on a die-struck or chiseled or engraved specimen. Also the surface of a cast object will show tiny pores and blemishes under high magnification, and these do not occur on hammered or struck surfaces.

Of course some objects originally were cast, including some buckles, buttons, most pewter pieces, and even some ancient coins. The task of distinguishing the fake from the original then becomes much more difficult. In such cases the loss of detail is a help. A specimen cast from the original mold will still be crisper than one cast in a mold made from an existing specimen. If the piece used by the faker to make his mold had seen any use, it would undoubtedly have acquired some scars along the way. Every piece made in the new mold would then have the same scars in the same place, and if one is lucky enough to see two pieces cast from that mold with the identical scars, the fraud is obvious. The chances of two objects, spoons or candlesticks, for instance, having acquired exactly the same scars independently are so remote as to be considered impossible. The same thing is true of pieces bearing stamped maker's marks or hallmarks. These were struck by hand after the object had been finished, and it would be rare indeed to find two pieces with the marks in exactly the same position and orientation and impressed to the same depth. If the faker uses an original mold—and a number of these still exist for buttons, spoons, ladles, plates, etc.—it is often impossible to spot a recent casting. You can only go by the patina, and frequently there is none, for collectors prefer to keep their pewter and silver bright. In such cases you can only look for signs of use —and cross your fingers!

SIGNS OF WEAR

As in wood, signs of wear and scars from use are helpful guides in separating the truly old from the modern fake. Iron and steel are hard metals, but even they are not immune from scratches and abrasion. Andirons, footed skillets and other objects which customarily rested on stone or brick hearths will always show wear on their feet. I have seen iron racks in which 18th-century smokers placed their clay pipes on the hearth to burn them clean with their flat "penny" feet almost completely worn away. Victorian cast iron boot jacks will show smooth areas on the high spots where the gentleman placed his "holding" foot when drawing the boot from his other foot. This is in contrast to the rest of the surface which almost always has the slightly matte finish of cast iron produced by the sand mold. It takes harsh abrasion or heavy pressure to produce such signs of wear on these hard metals, but if you look in the areas where evidence should be found, you can quite often find it.

Figure 67 (right top)

Diagram of engraving done with a hammer driven burin. The sectional view at the left shows the groove with the raised edges that this technique produces. The edges then must be polished off. This means that if there had been a scratch on the surface before the engraving, the polishing off of the raised edges would cause the scratch to appear to stop a short distance from the grooves. The sketch at right illustrates the appearance (much magnified) of a scratch that was on the surface before the engraving was done (left) and another scratch that came after the engraving and so goes right up to the cuts and possibly down into them.

Figure 68

The engraving at the top appears on the frame of an American Volcanic pistol of about 1855. Note the rather coarse sawtooth cuts typical of almost all American hammer driven engraving. The numerous blemishes and scratches that indicate true aging go right up to the edges of the cuts. The engraving below is a modern copy of the Volcanic engraving but done in an English style. The pitch of the cuts is smaller and indicates both a differently shaped tool and a different manner of holding it. The scratches that were on the plate before the engraving terminate a short distance from the cuts. Some more recent scratches go right up to them. *Courtesy Stanley M. Diefenthal.*

Figure 69 (right)
The name H. WATKEYS has been engraved on this genuine American musket of the Revolutionary War period in recent years. The style of letters is incorrect for the supposed period. The work is amateurish, and it seems to have been done with an electric vibra-tool causing all lines to end bluntly. *Courtesy the Smithsonian Institution.*

Figure 70 (bottom left)
A fake English drinking vessel of the 17th century. The shape is poor and the engraving is dreadful stylistically. *Courtesy the Victoria & Albert Museum, London. Crown Copyright.*

Figure 71
Fake of French late 17th century pewter ewer. The general shape, and the decoration, including the engraving, are bad, and the workmanship is poor. *Courtesy the Victoria & Albert Museum, London. Crown Copyright.*

The softer metals scratch and wear much more easily. The bases of candlesticks, the bottoms of grinding mortars, etc., should always show signs of wear. Normally these objects are not absolutely flat so there will be areas where slight pitting from the sand mold or patination in the file or lathe marks will still be visible, but the areas which come in contact with a table, floor or hearth should be polished smooth with some scratches caused by individual pieces of grit. If the feet or the bottom of the base are uniformly smooth and free from scratches or if the scratches are too regular, they might have been produced with abrasive paper in an effort to simulate real wear. With a magnifying glass you can see that the scratches from real wear are almost never exactly parallel or of the same width or depth. Each scratch is different from every other. It is almost impossible to reproduce their appearance artificially. There should also be a few nicks or scratches elsewhere on the surface. Mortars especially will show scratches and wear on the inside of the bottom and around the inside of the lip where the pestle has rubbed.

The softer metals also wear away when they are polished, and the conscientious housewife usually tried to keep her silver, brass and pewter gleaming. Over the years such polishing rounded the edges of facets, softened the contours of moldings, and sometimes almost obliterated engraving and touch marks. Hard sharp edges and crisp moldings are a sure sign that a piece has seen little use and almost no polishing. It is possible that it was purchased new and put away in a chest for 200 years, but the most likely explanation is that it is of very recent manufacture.

ENGRAVING

One of the more common types of faking involves the addition of engraved names, dates and decorations. There will be references to this throughout this chapter, but it might be well to discuss the topic in general here since its detection involves workmanship, patination and signs of wear. Engraving is accomplished by cutting grooves in metal with a sharp tool called a burin. The design of this tool has changed enough over the centuries for a skilled connoisseur to be able to note differences in the shape of the groove. Techniques of holding the tool and the metal to be engraved also vary by period and by schools of engravers. Recognizing these differences as well as period styles in ornament and lettering requires considerable study of authentic specimens.

When the burin is driven by a hammer, as in gun engraving, there is at least one ready guide that any collector with a good lens can detect readily. As the burin cuts its groove, it raises a burr on one or both sides of the cut. If the faker leaves this rough burr, it is an immediate sign of new workmanship. Thus he normally polishes it off. When he does so he interferes with the patination as mentioned previously. But he does more than this. He also obliterates any old scratches in the area he has polished away. Thus you should be sure to look carefully at any engraved design through a good lens. If a scratch stops short of the engraved cut and then picks up again a tiny distance on the other side of the cut, it means that the scratch was there before the engraving. A scratch that occurred after the engraving will run right into the edge of the cut. The only way a faker can avoid this tell-tale clue is to polish every single scratch and scar off the surface before engraving, and this normally produces even more obvious clues that indicate his dishonest activities. Jewelry engraving, unfortunately, is done with a soft touch and so does not leave a burr—if it is well done.

SILVER

Because of their rarity and value, antiques of silver have been faked and reworked more often and in more different ways than almost any other type of metalwork. Complete specimens have been newly made. Simple specimens have been converted into

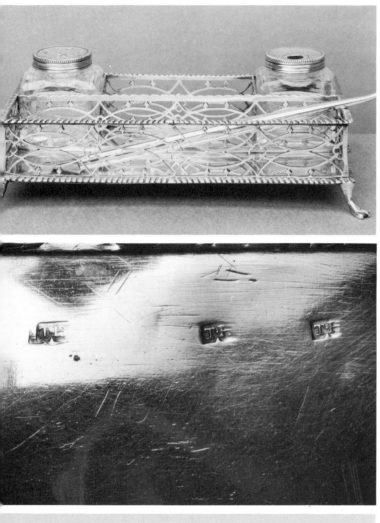

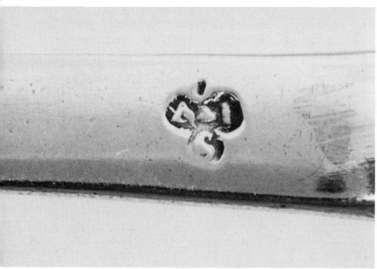

Figure 72 (top)
Silver standish or inkstand, c. 1760–1780, probably made in England. *Courtesy the Henry Francis du Pont Winterthur Museum, Study Colllection.*

Figure 73 (center)
Bottom of the inkstand in the previous illustration. A new sheet of silver, suitably nicked and scratched has been soldered over the original to hide the English marks, and fake touchmarks suggesting the piece was made by Thomas Hammersley of New York have been struck on it, interrupting the pattern of the scratches. *Courtesy The Henry Francis du Pont Winterthur Museum, Study Collection.*

Figure 74
Crudely faked mark of the silversmith Jacobus Vander Spiegel. It will not stand comparison with an original. *Courtesy The Henry Francis du Pont Winterthur Museum, Study Collection.*

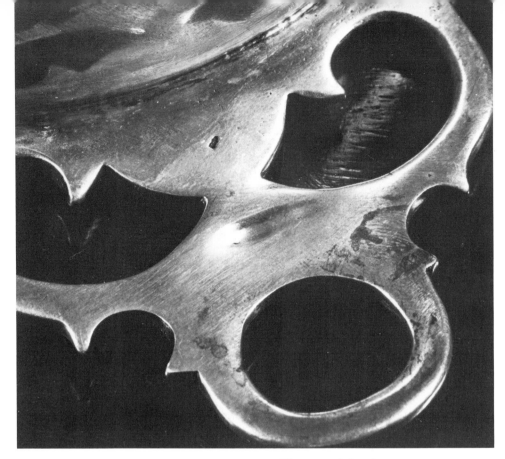

Figure 75 (above)
The handle of a silver porringer from which the touch mark has been burnished out as shown by the depression in the area between the three piercings.

Figure 76
Silver sugar bowl, Wilmington or Philadelphia, c. 1790. The monogram was engraved at that time, but the date 1776 was added about 1890 in a style improper for the 1776 date. *Collection of Charles G. Dorman.*

more desirable types. Unmarked specimens have had false marks added, and even marked pieces have had their marks removed or altered to increase their market value in a given country or area. All this is in addition to damaged objects which have been repaired or restored. The buyer of silver must therefore be especially wary.

Silver is a very soft metal, and consequently many pieces were damaged and repaired legitimately during their period of use. Handles on tankards and tea or chocolate pots sometimes pulled loose. Hollow handles sometimes suffered severe dents or broke. Hinges on lids occasionally wore out or snapped, and this sometimes led to the loss of the lid itself which had to be replaced. If the original maker also did the repair or replacement, it is almost impossible to detect it—and it makes little or no difference to the value of the piece. If the object had been in use for some time, and the repair was made by a different silversmith at a later date or in a different area, the replaced parts will reflect a different style. A Victorian spout, lid, handle or feet on an 18th-century teapot should be obvious to anyone with a slight knowledge of styles. Even if the restorer tried to imitate the design of the original, he seldom managed to do it exactly, and a comparison with an original—or sometimes with a good photograph of an original— will quickly reveal differences.

More insidious are changes designed to alter a simple piece into a more desirable and therefore more valuable type. Handles may be added to beakers that originally had none. Spouts may be added to cups or cans, and tankards or mugs that had no top may be given one. Again style is a good guide. So is the color of the metal. Most often the additions interfere visibly with the design of the piece, especially if there are engraved or embossed decorations. If a piece originally had handles or a spout, the maker would have taken them into consideration when he designed his decorations, and they would fit into it. No handle would ever solder on in the midst of an engraved design. The same is true of spouts—

and an added spout will be soldered on. The spouts of genuine pieces were formed in one piece with the body of the cup or beaker.

Solder joints are easy to detect. If lead solder has been used, it is immediately visible, but even silver solder can be seen if you use the proper techniques. There are always minute air holes left in soldering. They are ever so tiny, but if you blow on a suspected area so that the vapor in your breath condenses on the surface, the soldered area becomes visible. You can also obtain the same visibility by holding a white card or sheet of paper at right angles to the surface and reflecting the light on it.

The ability to find a soldered joint is especially important in cases where marks have been changed or added. Fakers have long made a practice of cutting an original mark out of an inexpensive item like a spoon or from a damaged specimen and soldering it into the bottom of an important piece such as a tankard or teapot. In this way they can convert an unmarked specimen into an apparently marked one, or increase the value of a marked one by substituting a more important name.

In addition to looking for the solder lines there are other clues you should consider in detecting a forgery. If the mark has been cut from a spoon, the metal will probably be thicker than the metal on a hollow piece such as a teapot. In such cases the forger has to thin his addition before soldering it in place. This frequently leads to a distortion of the mark or marks. Also there is always the most helpful of all guides—style. Is the style and workmanship of the piece in accordance with known pieces by the man whose mark it bears? There are times, in fact, when the criteria of style and workmanship are almost the only guides you have to go on. Very clever forgers have been known to electroplate a piece to which they have added a salvaged mark. This makes the solder joint very difficult or even impossible to detect, and if the mark has not been distorted by thinning, one must rely on style and the faintly different aura that electroplating gives to detect the forgery.

Sometimes a forger will make his own stamp. If he elects to create a mark for a silversmith whose name is known but whose mark is not recorded, you have to judge it generally by style. Are the letters the proper type for the period? Is the cartouche of an acceptable design and size? Sometimes a forger will work from the drawing of a mark in a book and will have little or no idea of the actual size of the original. In such instances a comparison with a genuine specimen bearing the same mark will quickly reveal the discrepancy. Genuine silversmiths' mark dies were cut from steel. They leave a sharp impression in details even when the surface is worn. The modern faker, if he cuts his own dies, usually makes them in copper, and these produce a softer outline. The same is true for a faker who makes a mold of an original mark and then casts a die. The crispness is lost. There is also another important clue left when a new mark is stamped on an old piece. The compression of the metal will interrupt the pattern of scratches on the original surfaces. As with wooden pieces, this is a warning that the mark was impressed after the scratches were made, usually a long time after.

Marks may be removed as well as added. For the American market, English or Continental marks may be polished out so that the piece may be sold at a higher price as an unmarked American specimen. On occasion a stolen object will have its mark removed to make identification more difficult. In such cases the depression created when the mark is removed is usually easy to see if you are careful to look for it. In some specialized forms, such as marrow spoons, the portion of the handle bearing the mark may be cut out, and the two ends joined together. Thus you should beware of any marrow spoon with a handle shorter than normal. This shortening is evidence of fraud even if the spoon has been electroplated. If it hasn't been, then the solder joint provides the *coup de grace* for the hoax.

As is the case with almost all other metal artifacts, silver pieces have been faked by making casts from original specimens. All the criteria mentioned previously about detecting casts apply to silver also, but there are a few specifics. Silver is so soft that it wears easily, and scratches even more easily. A cast will reproduce major wear, but it will not pick up the tiny scratches. Thus, if you see a tankard that has a badly worn thumb piece, but no scratches except those from polishing, turn your back on it immediately. Early silver spoons were normally hammered out. If you see such a spoon with any traces of the surface pitting found on a cast piece, it is immediately suspect. The placement of marks has been mentioned before, but on silver there are often more marks than on other metals—hallmarks, date letters, etc., as well as the maker's touch. These were seldom stamped in the same order or in exactly the same position so that two or three spoons in a set with identically ordered and spaced marks should be promptly rejected. Also there will usually be a roughness from the mold in the depressions of the mark where it is difficult to remove. Silver candlesticks were never originally made in one piece, and usually the metal was quite thin with a resin filler in the base to add weight and stability. A cast reproduction will always be made in one piece and usually of much thicker metal. Sometimes you even find them with solid bases, and this is an absolute indication of a fake. There should be solder lines on a candlestick, and the same is true of more complex pieces. Tea pots will have spouts soldered on, and if there are feet, these, too, will have been soldered in place. In a casting, normally all will be a single unit with no joints, although the complexities of mold making may require that a spout be cast separately and soldered on in the proper manner.

The metal itself is also a clue in judging the authenticity of a silver antique. The early silversmith worked from hammered sheet produced laboriously from an ingot. Despite his skill, the finished sheet is never of an absolutely uniform thickness. Modern fakers use rolled sheet silver for most of their work. It is absolutely uniform in thickness. Moreover, close examination of rolled sheet silver will reveal striations or "graining" produced by the great pressure under which it was manufactured. The alloy itself is also important. Almost all silver intended for use has some copper or other compatible metal added in order to harden it. Wide variance from the norms expected for "sterling" or "coin" silver can be detected by weight or by eye, but minor variations require spectographic analysis. It is even possible to be reasonably sure whether a piece of silver originated in England or America by the amount of copper in the alloy. Spectrographic analyses are expensive and their results require expert interpretation, but if you are contemplating the expenditure of $10,000 or more on an important piece of silver, it would be worthwhile to incur the added expense.

Plain pieces of silver are frequently "improved" by the addition of engraving. Sometimes it may be a decorative design, sometimes a crest, or even a family name or initials. Here style is the primary aid in detection. Few engravers know period style well enough to copy it convincingly, and a remarkable number of them seem entirely innocent of important characteristics. They forget, for instance, that 18th-century block letters almost always had serifs, and they misunderstand the shading frequently found on letters of that era. Also, they commonly forget to allow for a mark, if one appears on the visible surface of a piece. These marks were always struck after the piece was completed, and they never interfered with the decoration. If you find a piece with a stamped mark in the midst of a decorated area, something is definitely wrong. Then there is the matter of wear. Old engraving will always feel soft and smooth. There should be no sharp edges or burrs. Sometimes, thoughtless descendants will have their own initials engraved on inherited family silver. I have seen such initials and even commemorative or presentation inscriptions in the so-called Old English lettering popular in the late 19th century on genuine 18th-century silver. In such cases there was no intention of fraud, but the value of the piece has been lessened and so you should be alert for it.

A variant of true silver is Sheffield plate. This is a process invented in the 18th century by which thin sheets of silver were bonded to a copper body. To the best of my knowledge there has been little faking of Sheffield objects, but when it has been done it is seldom convincing. The silver sheets on the outside surfaces are very thin and wear off on the high spots after years of use and polishing. Frequently an unscrupulous dealer will try to improve a piece of Sheffield by electroplating it, but the weight is different from true silver. It is often lighter because the copper is harder and tougher than silver and so thinner sheets could be used. Most British-made pieces will be properly marked as silver, Sheffield plate or electroplate, and so these marks have to be removed before replating, and this defacement should be apparent. American pieces often were not marked in the early years, and thus this clue is absent.

CANDLESTICKS AND ANDIRONS

Among the metal objects that have attracted the attention of fakers on a large scale in recent years are brass candlesticks. Such sticks have been faked and altered for a long, long time, but the last twenty years have seen the incidence of such chicanery increase at an astounding rate because of the growing interest in these pieces among collectors. The most common techniques employed by the fraudulent fabricators of antique candlesticks are the marriage of parts from two different sticks and the casting of new sticks from another specimen. Sometimes they have combined both techniques with laughable results. An example of this can be found in a pair of candlesticks that found their way into the collections at Independence National Historical Park many years ago. One of the sticks had been composed of a vertical element with candle socket of the mid-18th century and a base from the very early 18th century. The marriage was immediately apparent because of the incompatibility of the two styles even though the faker had ground the drip pan off the socket. The other stick was

Figure 77 (right)
Candlestick composed of elements from two different sticks. The base dates about 1700, the vertical member is probably early 19th century. A trained eye should immediately notice the difference in styles, but even a beginner should realize that a drip pan on the socket would make the drip pan in the base redundant.

Figure 78 (bottom left)
"Pair" of candlesticks in the Independence Hall study collection. The stick on the left is composed of a sophisticated vertical member of a later date than the simple base. The base and column do not match in color, but the man who "married" them did realize that the drip pan on the socket was redundant, and so he ground it off. The stick on the right was cast from the one on the left and is made all in one piece. *Courtesy Independence National Historical Park.*

Figure 79
The socket and drip pan of a mid 18th century candlestick. The brazed seam uniting the two halves can be seen as a vertical line inside the socket.

Figure 80 (top)
Mid 18th century candlestick with a replaced top. The stick is original up to the top of the baluster. The part above is modern, and the "restorer" not only failed to match the original part in color but also failed to repeat any of the design elements. The new portion also lacks the scars that cover the surface of the lower three-quarters of the stick.

Figure 81
Base of a fake candlestick, supposedly about 1700. The raised circular area at about the four o'clock position is the spot where the casting sprue was cut off. Just above and to the right is a flow area superimposed over the concentric circular marks left when the original piece was finished on a lathe. Thus it is obvious that this specimen is cast from an original.

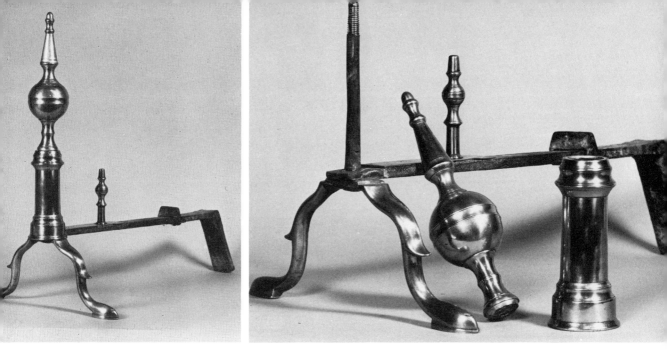

Figure 82 (above left)
Brass andiron of about 1800 with typical iron log support.

Figure 83 (above right)
The andiron in the previous illustration with the finial and column dis-assembled.

Figure 84 (bottom left)
Back leg of the iron log support showing the surface characteristics produced by long contact with fire.

Figure 85
The vertical iron rod on this andiron of about 1810–1820 is even more roughly forged than the one on the previous specimen.

a direct cast from the first one, made in one piece, which would not have been done, and showing the same scars in exactly the same places. No reasonably astute connoisseur should ever have been fooled, but someone was.

Early candlesticks were seldom made in one piece, to the best of my knowledge. If you find one, it is either an unusual specimen or a fake. After about 1680 the brass founders who manufactured candlesticks normally used half-patterns for the vertical column and candle socket. They hollowed out these patterns so that the stick itself would be hollow, save previous metal, and produce a lighter stick. Core casting to produce a hollow stick was little understood and seldom used until the end of the 18th century. When the founder had cast the two halves of the column he brazed them together. This results in two vertical seams directly opposite each other on the vertical member. Sometimes you can find these seams, but often they are very difficult or even impossible to see even using the condensed vapor from breath or the reflected light from a white card in the manner you would employ for detecting soldered joints in silver. After brazing the founder polished the piece on a lathe and attached it to a separately cast base, usually by means of a rivet or by cutting screw threads. The exception to these comments may be found in some Continental European sticks. I have seen some genuine 18th-century specimens from Spain, Portugal and the Netherlands, and even a few English examples, that had core-cast columns and cups. In the English specimens it is usually only the smaller sticks that are made in this fashion.

If the faker attaches a vertical member of one style to the base of another, as in the case of the Independence National Historical Park pieces mentioned above, the aberration gives the fraud away immediately. If he is more knowledgeable (or luckier) and uses elements that are compatible in size and style, there are still clues that may reveal his nefarious activities. For one thing, a founder normally cast a run of candlesticks from the same pot of alloy.

Thus the exact mixture of copper and tin or zinc should be found in both base and column. Minute differences would be detectable only through spectrographic analysis, but any significant change will produce a difference in color. Thus if one part is bright yellow and the other slightly reddish, you know right away that they were not cast from the same pot. It is possible that a founder might have an extra base or two on hand and add the upright portions from another day's pouring. He might also get his alloy too hot and "boil" out some of the tin during a run, but the chances for this are slight, and the chances that there would be a visible difference in color in parts assembled by the same founder are slighter still. These color differences, incidentally, are normally much harder to detect when the metal is brightly polished. I was fooled in this way a few years ago. The gleaming stick was in proper style throughout, and I could see no color differences. After I had had the stick for several months and the luster began to fade, I noted to my chagrin that the base was noticeably redder than the shaft. Then I noticed, too, that the moldings at the joint were just a tiny fraction out of line. The mis-alignment was very very slight, but combined with the color difference it was enough to damn the piece—and increase my collection of fakes.

This brings up the other clues to look for in determining if the base and shaft of a candlestick began life together. Look at the rivet in the inside of the base that often attaches the shaft. Is it an old rivet—smooth and patinated the same as the rest of the base cavity? Or is it bright with some rough sharp edges? On the outside, is the shaft exactly centered on the base? If there are moldings at the joint, do they jibe? Is there any awkwardness in design? Can you see any trace on the top of the base around the joint where a shaft of slightly different diameter or shape once fit? Normally this will show up as a slight difference in patination or surface texture. If any of these signs appear, it is cause to think long and hard before investing. If they are all there, you should reject the stick without further thought.

Finally, the surfaces of both the shaft and the base should show the same amount of wear from polishing, and the same sort of scars from abuse. This is not to say that both pieces should have an absolutely equal number of nicks, dents and scratches, but if the shaft has been knocked about a good deal, the base should not be almost pristine. And if the moldings have been considerably rounded from polishing on one element, they should not be crisp on the other.

Another minor clue to look for is a socket that is smoothed inside. Early craftsmen customarily finished the socket so there would be no roughness that would make it difficult to remove the butt of the candle. Modern casters sometimes forget this.

The signs of age which you should look for on brass or bronze andirons are very similar to those on candlesticks, but there are also some additional clues. First of all, there should be signs of severe wear on the feet. Hearths are notoriously rough and abrasive and the bottoms of the feet should show evidence of long contact with such a surface, even on the iron foot at the back end of the log support. Also the iron log support, which should show signs of hand forging, should also bear evidence of contact with fire. This produces a scale and sometimes a lifting away of the surface that are quite easily recognized once you have looked at a few. It should be remembered, however, that these supports sometimes "burned out" through long use and had to be replaced. At the front end of the log support a forged rod was riveted in place to pass up through the brass elements that formed the decorative front feet and shaft of the andiron. This iron rod should be roughly square in section or square with chamfered corners, and the top end should have coarse threads cut with a die for attaching the finial.

The brass elements consisted usually of three or possibly four pieces—the feet, which were usually riveted in place by the iron upright rod, the shaft and the finial. The shaft was always hollow and made in two pieces like the shaft of a candlestick. The finial, if large, would also be in two pieces, and it would be tapped to screw onto the iron rod. With luck you should be able to find the brazed joints on both the shaft and the finial. On square shafts, the joints are normally on two opposite corners, and these are harder to see than the joints on the opposite sides of a round shaft. Earlier andirons are apt to be lighter than later ones as the founder sought to conserve metal, but this is difficult to gauge except after long experience. The legs and feet may be hollowed out in back and not fully round, but this is never the case with the shaft and finial.

Cast or wrought-iron andirons are much harder to judge than the brass variety. Here one can only look for wear on the feet, patination, and the method of attaching the log support. The latter may, in fact, be cast in place. Be especially careful of cast iron specimens that have been painted. The heat from the fire would have scorched or burned off paint, and so these iron andirons were not usually painted in the period when they were intended for use. It is always possible that some misguided person has painted an old pair of andirons in recent years to make them, in his view, more decorative. Then one has to check the surface underneath the paint to see if there is any trace of genuine oxidation. Active or recent rust is red. Later comes the black ferroferric oxide, popularly called millscale or "inactive rust" which cannot be produced quickly and easily. Even a year of lying in the open will not produce it. Thus the faker usually hopes that the red rust will satisfy the prospective customer, but to be sure, he may resort to paint or the technique of applying a coat of linseed oil and burning it off. The latter technique produces a nice black color, but it does not give the proper surface texture. Nor will it produce the proper appearance of long direct contact with fire on the log supports.

BELT BUCKLES, BUTTONS, HAT PLATES AND HORSE BRASSES

Small, highly desirable items such as belt and hat plates, buckles, buttons and horse brasses have attracted the attention of the faker at least since the turn of the century, but the years since 1960 have seen the production of fraudulent specimens increase phenomenally. In part this has been caused by the recent centennial of the American Civil War and the anticipation of the Revolutionary War bicentennial, but the scarcity of original objects and the rapidly growing number of collectors are also significant factors. Demand is such that some Confederate belt buckles now command $800 or more, and this presents a great temptation to unscrupulous craftsmen since they can be reproduced very easily. All of these artifacts can be manufactured quickly by any reasonably skilled craftsman, and even if few other categories command the price of a Confederate buckle, the profit ratio is very good indeed.

For a cast specimen, all a forger needs is an original piece to work from. From this he makes his mold and casts fakes as rapidly as he can market them. To detect such a fraud, all you can rely on is patination, signs of wear and the appearance on the market of a number of specimens with the same nicks and scars that happen to have been on the original. The patinating techniques have been discussed at the beginning of this chapter. Wear will be found on the loops where the leather of the belt fastened, and, in two-piece buckles, the area of the tongue and slot. Look especially in the corners of the belt loops. Fakers often fail to burnish this area as smooth as they should. Leather rubbing against brass will produce a very soft smooth surface and rounded corners.

Sometimes fakers have set out to produce entirely new belt buckles of their own design. No one had ever seen a Confederate Marine Corps buckle, for instance, and then within a two week period four of them appeared in shops in the Washington, D.C.

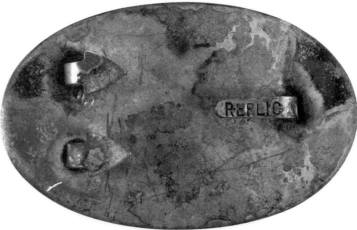

Figure 86 (top)
Fake buckle purporting to be for the 3rd Regiment of Artillery, early 19th century. The design is imaginary, the engraving terrible with no resemblance to period style. *Courtesy Robert H. McCauley.*

Figures 87 A & B
Front and back of a reproduction U.S. waistbelt buckle of the Civil War period with lead filled back. This one is properly made. It is also deeply stamped REPLICA. Not all of the current reproductions are so honestly marked. *Courtesy the Smithsonian Institution.*

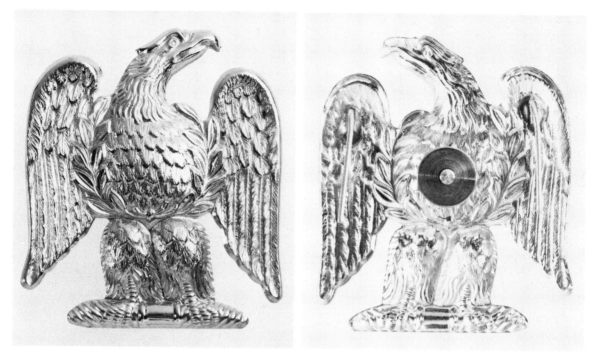

Figures 88 A & B (above)
Stamped reproduction of a U.S. Dragoons cap plate of 1833. The stamping is good, but fortunately the fastener on the back is completely wrong. *Courtesy the Smithsonian Institution.*

Figures 89 A & B
Stamped reproduction of the rare cap insignia for the United States Scouts. Again the fastener is incorrect. *Courtesy the Smithsonian Institution.*

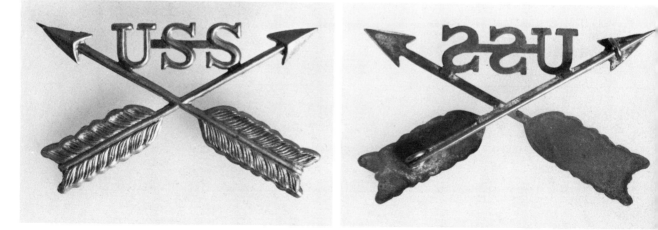

Figures 90 A & B (above)
"Reproduction" of a Confederate Naval officer's belt plate. The design is unknown among surviving original plates. The construction is not proper for the period, and the firm name "ISSAC & CO" is a misspelling. *Courtesy the Smithsonian Institution.*

Figure 91 (right)
"Reproduction" of the so-called Wells Fargo "Founders" belt plate. No such plate ever existed at the time. *Photo Courtesy* American Collector Magazine.

Figures 92 A & B
A specimen of one of the Wells Fargo "Founders" belt plates that has been artificially patinated to suggest that it has been excavated. The back is marked "TIFFANY/NEW YORK." Actually Tiffany never made any belt buckles for Wells Fargo. *Courtesy the Smithsonian Institution.*

Figure 93 (above)
According to the Wells Fargo Company the one and only belt plate ever produced for the Company is this specimen, adopted in 1973 after the furor caused by all the "reproductions." *Photo Courtesy* American Collector Magazine.

Figure 94 (center)
Two modern reproductions of horse brasses. The detail is bad, the casting and finishing are poor, and there are absolutely no signs of wear.

Figure 95
Back of one of the horse brasses in the previous illustration. It is completely unfinished, the edges of the holes are rough, and, of course, there are no signs of wear.

area. This sudden quantity of a previously unknown buckle plus its improbable design were sufficient to make all knowledgeable students skeptical.

Even die-struck hat and belt plates no longer present the production problem they once did. A faker can take an original plate and make a die with epoxy in the same way he would make a plaster of paris mold. An epoxy die is not as strong as a steel die, but it will usually be good for up to 100 strikes and then a new die can be made overnight. Good steel dies copying historic plates have also been produced recently in Hong Kong and Great Britain. In some instances the fakers have worked from the excellent scaled photographs in a book on American military insignia published by the Smithsonian Institution. Fortunately, however, the photographs did not show the backs of the plates, and the fakers had to invent their own fasteners which happily did not correspond to the fastening devices on the originals.

Some fakers have taken pains to stamp their buckles and buttons with makers' or dealers' names of the proper period. For some reason, however, these have usually been misspelled. The name Isaacs in the English firm of Isaacs & Company or S. Isaacs Campbell & Co. was misspelled "Issac." Courtney & Tennant was changed to "Courtney & Tennet." This may represent carelessness or there may be some legal reason for it in case the perpetrators of these hoaxes should be brought to court. Another common marking error is found on the buckles copying those used on the belt for the U. S. model 1832 Roman pattern foot artillery sword. These fakes are stamped "Dingee" or "R. D. & Co." Actually Robert Dingee never made any buckles. He produced only the leather work and stencilled his name on the inside of the belt itself. Rarely did he stamp a buckle. In recent years Wells Fargo belt buckles have joined the military types as popular objects for the faker, and a host of them have appeared on the market since 1970. There is even a completely fraudulent buckle supposedly given to Congressmen who rode on the Lincoln funeral train.

A special feature of many of these fake buttons and buckles, especially those produced by British makers, is that they come complete with a story of their having been found in an old chest in the basement of the original manufacturer. One purveyor, giving a corporate name with a London address and an impressive letterhead, advertised by direct mail and in publications that he had discovered such a cache of American Civil War buttons "down in a musty cellar" of an old manufacturing company in that city. Since this firm had made buttons for the Confederacy it sounded logical enough, but one look at the buttons themselves aroused suspicions even though they were well done. Students pooled their resources to do some investigating. The first startling fact that they discovered was that the firm sending out the advertisements was not listed in the London telephone directory even though it claimed to be a supplier to almost every maharajah in India. The next discovery was that the purported address of the firm proved to be a vacant lot. Finally, a correspondent approached the manufacturing company itself and talked with an executive who was a direct descendant of one of the men who founded the company in the 1790's. He stated categorically that no such cache of buttons had ever been found in any of their "musty cellars." That would seem to be the end of it, but one still occasionally sees one of the spurious buttons in collections.

Other false stories about the discovery of objects in basements or remote corners of warehouses have not been as easy to disprove. In some instances old and respected firms seem actually to be co-operating with the fakers. Original dies have been used, and inquiries to the firms have produced replies that are equivocal or evasive. In another instance a book was published to establish the "authenticity" of a series of buckles, but it was so bad that it has now become a collector's item as a wonderful example of unintentional humor. It gives dates for buckles earlier than features which appear in the design were built, and it even confuses a

Figure 96

Three cast reproductions of early coins. The two on the left are copies of the American pewter dollar of 1776, the specimen on the extreme left being especially well done and not intended for sale. Only four were made, but one was sold by an unscrupulous recipient and so the maker called back the other three and stamped them deeply on the edge. The second pewter dollar is a commercial reproduction of lesser quality. The coin at the right copies a Spanish silver "pillar dollar" of 1749. The metal is wrong, and it is obviously a cast instead of a stamping as the original was.

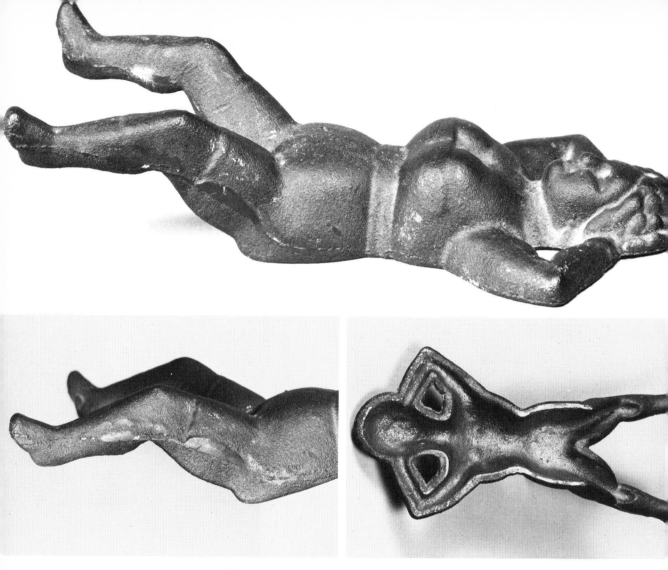

Figure 97 (top)
An orginal of the Victorian "naughty lady" bootjack which has been copied in huge quantities during the last quarter century. It does not show in the illustration, but there is old wear on the nose caused by pressure from the holding foot. The mold seam can be seen running along the side of the leg.

Figure 98 (above left)
Detail of the mold seam showing that it was smoothed by hand with a file. Most reproductions have had the seam smoothed with a high speed grinding wheel.

Figure 99
Underneath view of the bookjack showing the dull "pewter" color and the complete lack of paint which one normally finds covering all surfaces of the reproductions. Note also the bright areas of wear on the high spots along the edges caused by friction on the floor.

world famous designer of glass with a great company which manufactured jewelry, naming him as the maker of the plates.

Although some fake buttons, such as the purported London-made Confederate type mentioned above, have been die-struck, most fake buttons are casts. Usually the originals that they imitate were cast also, so you have to look for signs of wear, loss of detail and proper patination. Most button fakers seem to have a preference for either liver of sulphur or black paint to produce a semblance of patination, and these can be detected easily by their characteristics as noted at the beginning of the chapter.

Horse brasses have been a popular item in antique shops for many decades. Students generally agree that real faking of these objects began in the early 1920's. Fortunately, horse brasses followed an easily established pattern of manufacturing techniques and alloys that allow the student to note quickly if the brass he is offered conforms in weight, color and method of manufacture to the norm. It is almost impossible for the faker to obtain an alloy that corresponds even approximately to the pinchbeck or brilliant Walsall metals or the rolled spelter brass used at Walsall and Birmingham in the second half of the last century and the early 1900's. Once the collector has familiarized himself with the look and feel of these metals he can easily eliminate the greater portion of fakes. There are several good published accounts of the evolution of horse brasses which outline the designs and methods of manufacture to be expected from the various periods of their existence, and these, too, will help eliminate many of the frauds.

Aside from these guides, you can always study the brass itself. A few fakes are handmade from rolled sheet brass, but most are cast and artificially patinated. If they are offered in a polished condition, look at the strap loops. Long years of wear against leather will have smoothed the inner edges of a loop in a way that most fakers fail to simulate convincingly. Also the fakes often fail to show proper wear along the back of the lower edge of the brass which often makes these edges considerably thinner than the rest of the brass. There should also be an occasional nick or scratch as well as a silky finish of tiny scratches produced by long years of hand polishing.

COINS

Coins have been faked from antiquity, usually with the intent to use them as currency rather than for the later collector. In fact, some of the ancient forgeries have more value today than the coins they attempted to simulate. During the course of history coins have been both cast and struck, and the connoisseur should know which technique would be proper for the coin he is examining. He should also know the proper metal, and the quality of the metal. Most modern fakes of coins are casts, and these can be detected by examining the surface under magnification to pick up the tiny bubbles and pits that typify a casting as well as the loss of detail and crispness that must result when a cast is made from another coin. False patination is another clue, and you should make sure that if a portion of the design is blurred from wear, the entire surface is as smooth as it should be from the constant rubbing that produced the wear. Sometimes you can detect facets on the edge from careless filing of mold seams. Once in a great while you may encounter a fake coin made from a new die. This usually happens only in the case of very rare and expensive pieces. In such cases the first thing to do is to check the suspected coin against an original to see if there are any aberrations in workmanship or design. Then look for wear and other signs of use as well as patination. An apparently mint uncirculated pine tree shilling or a Bermuda hog penny or any other such early rarity should give a prospective buyer "pause with cause."

CAST IRON OBJECTS

Among the cast iron objects that have been reproduced or faked in quantity over the years have been mechanical banks, toys,

Figure 100 (top left)

Tinned iron primer box about 1861. Note that the tin on the front of the box has oxidized unevenly. The horizontal patterns indicate the ripples where the tin dripped off when the sheet iron was lifted from the melted tin. The lighter areas are where the tin was thickest. All tin has disappeared from the latch and the rim from constant abrasion on those areas. Although the inside of the box top looks black from refracted light, it retains almost all its original tin coating and is very bright.

Figure 101 (top right)

Modern reproduction of a tin candle sconce. The maker apparently used a machine-made tin plate and riveted his strap and candle holder to it poorly. Then he used a dip of acid or lye to produce a very unconvincing overall rust pattern.

Figure 102 (bottom left)

The back of a relatively recent tin candle sconce, perhaps 50 years old. The dark areas within the inner circle are rust caused by the use of an acid flux for the solder.

Figure 103

Painted tin cigar box, probably French, of the early 19th century. The evidence of age appears mostly along the edge. The red brown paint has chipped off in a number of areas. Where this has happened relatively recently the tin remains and produces the irregular white areas. The slightly darker areas are oxidized tin, and the rough dark areas are corroded iron where both paint and tin have been gone for a long time. It is this combination of different stages of damage that offers convincing evidence of the age of painted tinware.

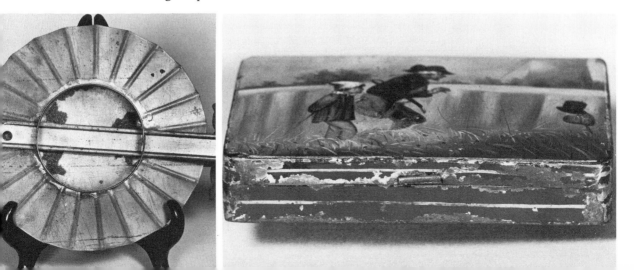

bootjacks, hitching posts and trivets. Some, such as the hitching posts, are almost impossible to authenticate if they have been cast from an original, painted many times and left in the open for twenty or more years on someone's lawn. Generally speaking, however, recent pieces are not so well finished as older ones. Labor costs are much higher now, and less time is spent in hand work. Also modern casting sand tends to be coarser than the sand used a century or more ago. This gives a much more pebbled surface, and even when painted the surface is not as smooth as on truly old specimens. Finally, in most instances the reproductions are lighter in weight than the originals. With banks and many toys you can look inside and see the bare surface of the metal. If old, it will be matte but not really pebbled. Also it will be a dull pewter color with maybe some slight rusting, though this is not usual. It should not be bright, and the insides should never be painted. The outside paint when used should show signs of age, and it should be very hard and worn off in spots with rusted iron showing on a relatively smooth surface. Items designed for outdoor use should have many coats of hard paint. Some objects should also show signs of wear, such as the feet of trivets that stood on a hearth, the pressure points on a bootjack and the hole in the hitching post where the ring is attached.

TINWARE

Authentic old tinware is one of the most difficult of all antiques for the connoisseur to distinguish. It was made legitimately for a great many years. It has also been reproduced for more than seventy years, and a number of very competent craftsmen are working in the field today, using traditional techniques and, unfortunately, often adding false signs of antiquity. Still there are some clues you can look for that will help eliminate the products of all but the most skillful and patient of fakers.

Tinware is actually sheet iron with a thin coating of tin on each side. The earliest sheets were small, usually 10 x 14 inches, and produced by dipping the sheets of rolled iron into melted tin. As objects made from these sheets aged, the tin oxidized or wore off. When it wore off the iron rusted. Except when a tinned object was scoured, the rust usually appeared in tiny dots which then increased in size and gradually covered whole areas. This is one of the primary things to look for. A tinned piece does not rust uniformly all over. Neither does it oxidize uniformly. Protected areas will retain much of the tin and stay reasonably bright. The backs of candle sconces that hung against the wall, for instance, usually retain considerably more unoxidized tin than the fronts. The corners of interior angles normally retain more than the flat exposed surfaces, and so on. A faker usually creates his patina by dipping his work in a chemical which either removes some or all of the tin or deposits a coating. When he does this he produces a uniform color on the entire piece. Often it is a dark unsightly gray that looks quite different from the true gray tin oxide, and this is an immediate sign of fakery. If he uses an acid, the cut edges where the iron comes in direct contact with the solution will turn a bright red from rust. The solder joints also should never be the same color as the tinned surfaces. Always look to make sure that an originally tinned object has oxidized or the iron beneath rusted in a natural and logical way for the type of use it would have had, and that the solder is clearly visible and of a natural color. If the maker used an acid flux for his solder and failed to wash it off well, an area of rust will quickly develop. Old craftsmen sometimes used acid fluxes, too, but usually they were more careful to neutralize it. If they hadn't, an old piece will probably have rusted right through by this time. If a large area of bright tin remains, hold it to your eye and look along the surface. Often you can sight ripple or sag lines where the tin ran when the plate was lifted from the tinning pot. Some fake tinware is made of iron coated with an alloy of tin and base metal. It never was bright and shiny like real tin plate. Thus you will not be able to find even a tiny bright area.

Painted tinware, or tole as it is sometimes called, presents an entirely different set of problems and of clues. Originally, the tin painters coated the product with a black bituminous asphaltum varnish which they dried under controlled temperatures. Later asphaltum varnishes in other colors appeared. On top of this ground the decorator added his designs in paint or metallic leaf, most frequently gold. These paints have a distinct feel and appearance which you can learn to recognize by studying authentic specimens. There is usually a translucence when grounds other than black were used. Style, also, is helpful. Each principal center of production—Berlin, Connecticut in the United States or Pontypool or Bilston in England, for instance, developed designs and brush techniques which make their products quickly identifiable to the trained eye. In recent years the painting of tinware has become a popular avocation, and the students who pursue it often become very skillful in imitating styles and techniques. There is no intent to deceive in their efforts, and they often sign their products, but an unscrupulous person can remove or paint over such signatures. When this has been done, you have to look for other signs of authenticity.

Fortunately they exist. Few painted objects have survived the years unscathed. There will be dents, scratches, and areas where paint has been knocked off. Scratches and other accidents which remove paint frequently remove the tin too, and then the iron core begins to rust. If damaged areas have been painted in or a signature removed or painted over, this will become immediately visible under ultra-violet light. The new paint will fluoresce entirely differently from the old, usually showing up as dark blotches. Thus an ultra-violet lamp is an essential tool for any collector of painted tin.

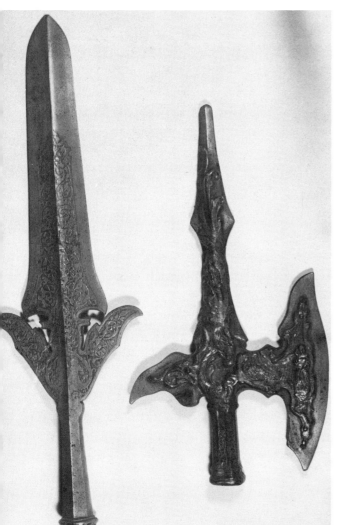

Figure 104 (top)
Two polearm heads of cast iron made for the decoration of Victorian mansions. *James D. Forman Collection.*

Figure 105 (center right)
Dagger decorated in late 19th century style that for many years passed as "early Roman." *James D. Forman Collection.*

Figure 106 (bottom left)
Helmet, probably by Hans Maistetter of Innsbruck shortly after 1500. Note that the eye slots are absolutely straight. Just above the visor are two slightly damaged places which show the laminated structure of the metal.

Figure 107
A detail from the back of the Maistetter helmet which clearly shows the lamination of the metal.

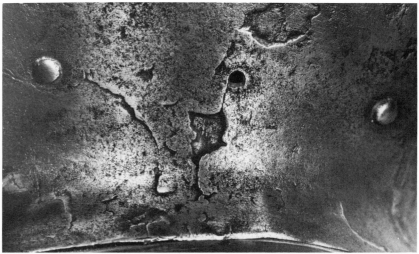

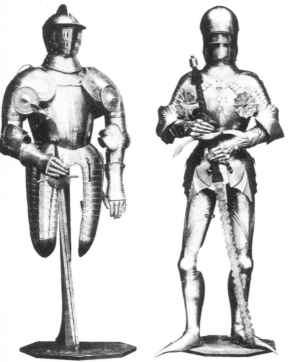

Figure 108 (above left)
Interior of a 16th century burgonet helmet. Note that the skull was made in one piece with only the hinged cheek pieces separate. The hammer marks are clearly visible, including the marks of the embossing tool that formed the roped comb in the center. The irregular straight lines around the bottom are stretch marks created when the metal was thinned and stretched out for a flaring base. *Bluford W. Muir Collection.*

Figure 109 (above)
Modern fake of a 16th century combless morion. The shape is poor, and the helmet is made in two pieces with a weak soldered seam. Although it is not visible in the picture, the metal is modern rolled sheet iron.

Figure 110
Two reproduction suits of armor offered for sale by Ernst Schmidt of Munich early in this century. These are better than most commercially reproduced suits, but there are sufficient errors in style, material and workmanship to permit students to recognize them quickly for what they are. From *Arms—Armor from the Atelier of Ernst Schmidt-Munich* by E. Andrew Mowbray. *Courtesy of the author.*

Figure 111 (*top*)
Genuine 16th century burgonet "improved" by etching in the Victorian period. The style of the etching is very obviously mid-19th century and completely wrong for the 16th century. *Bluford W. Muir Collection.*

Figure 112 (*center*)
Genuine 16th century morion-cabasset that has been embossed in the 19th century to enhance its value. Again the stylistic errors give it away as do the signs of reworking found on the interior. *Courtesy the Victoria & Albert Museum, London. Crown Copyright.*

Figure 113
Etching from the blade of a 17th century Italian gunner's stiletto. The lettering style and degraded Latin are correct for the period, but even better evidence of age is the fact that the corrosion has taken place after the etching was done, almost obliterating some lines and letters.

Figure 114 (top left)
Fake cup-hilted rapier made in the 19th century. The design is poor. Both ends of the cross guard turn up which they would never have done. Finally both pommel and guard are made of cast iron. On an original they would have been wrought iron. *Courtesy the Victoria & Albert Museum, London. Crown Copyright.*

Figure 115 (top right)
Fake cup-hilted rapier. The grips are much too long and the cross guard does not rest on the cup (which is improperly proportioned). The blade is a travesty. Workmanship and design do not match. It is, in fact, the kind of horror that should never fool anyone, but the previous owner apparently was. *Courtesy James D. Forman.*

Figure 116 (center)
The tang rivet on this sword of about 1500 has never been tampered with. The corrosion matches that of the rest of the pommel and has built up around the edges of the rivet so that it is difficult to see the junction.

Figure 117
The blade of this early 17th century English basket-hilted broad sword has been removed to fix the grips in recent years. The sword was then reassembled and the tang re-riveted. The rivet is amateurish, rough, and the patina does not match that of the pommel.

ARMS AND ARMOR

Arms and armor have been faked in some quantity at least since the 18th century, but it was during the gothic revival, beginning late in the second quarter of the last century, that production of spurious medieval and renaissance armor and weapons began in earnest. The interest in gothic architecture, the building of new castles and the refurbishing of old ones led to a demand for suits of armor and for panoplies of arms for decoration and atmosphere. Usually the arms were swords or polearms. Faked firearms came later in the 19th century when wealthy amateurs began to add finely decorated weapons to their art collections. Then the great increase in all forms of arms collecting that developed about 1900 and has increased steadily ever since has provided the inspiration and market for a whole host of unscrupulous craftsmen.

Some of the early fakes of armor have been around long enough to acquire quite genuine patina, and you can only detect them by style, workmanship and materials. Fortunately this is often fairly easy. Samuel Pratt, the famous English dealer—and faker—turned out quantities of reworked authentic bits of armor as well as fakes made from scratch. His knowledge of style, however, was abysmal. Although his ridiculous great helms occasionally still turn up as illustrations in books and on dealers' shelves, no connoisseur who has familiarized himself with the appearance and construction of authentic specimens should ever be fooled. For one thing, any piece of genuine armor should always be anatomically correct and functional, in addition to following the period style in form. If a helmet designed to rest upon the shoulders has its eye slots so high that it would require a man with a 12-inch neck and a very low forehead to see through them, it is immediately suspect. Also, eye slots—or "occularia" as the learned curators like to call them—should always be in a straight horizontal line. Otherwise the wearer would have no lateral vision. In fact, he might not be able to see at all if the slots did not happen to cross one or both eyes at some point. This seems like a very obvious thing, but the number of helmets with slanted vision slots, especially on the bellows visors of early 16th-century style, that one finds on the market is astounding. You should apply this same criterion of anatomical feasibility to all the other elements in a suit of armor. Could a man actually move in it? Many people have the false impression that a suit of armor was a clumsy thing, and that movements were greatly restricted. This is absolutely false. Real armors were beautifully designed to give considerable freedom of movement. They were anything but clumsy and awkward. Modern tests show beyond a shadow of doubt that a man in a properly fitted armor can do anything he could do in an overcoat. Some special purpose armors, such as those for jousting or siege work, restricted the movements of their wearers, but they are the exceptions. Generally speaking, if you are offered a piece of armor that does not allow for every possible movement of the part of the body it was designed to protect, you should be highly suspicious.

Other good guides to authenticity are workmanship and materials. The plates from which armor was constructed were hammered out by hand. They vary in thickness, and usually you can see hammer and chasing tool marks on the inside. Some of the variations in thickness result from hand work, but often the differences are part of the design to give greater protection in exposed areas while less vulnerable places are thinner to reduce weight. Thus the comb and top of a helmet skull are thicker than the sides. The center of a breastplate is thicker than the areas under the arms. Breastplates are normally heavier than backplates, and so on. There are exceptions, of course, but real armor was never made of absolutely uniform rolled sheet iron or steel like those now being made in Spain offered for sale as decorator items by some large department stores. Another sign of old metal is that it often has a laminated structure, and if you look closely you can usually find a tiny crack on the outer or inner surface where the top layer has separated from the one beneath. Finally, one other good guide is the construction of the skull or bowl of a helmet. Early bowls were almost always made in one piece. This required great skill on the part of the armorer, and only a few fakers have been able to duplicate the feat. Thus most spurious helmets are made in two pieces joined down the center of the crown from front to back. It is true that later and cheaper helmets were often originally made this way—as a rule from the late 16th century on. But the joint was always a strong one. Usually the armorer riveted the two pieces together at the front and back and crimped and welded the seam along the comb. He never used a simple soldered or brazed joint that would have come apart after one good sword blow.

There have been a few superb armorers in the last seventy or eighty years. Mostly they have worked for such firms as Ernst Schmidt in Munich (whose catalog has recently been reprinted) or for the great collectors such as William Randolph Hearst or for some of the great museums. One or two of them had very forgiving consciences, but most of them offered their products honestly as reproductions (for example, Schmidt's atelier) or as repairs or restorations to incomplete specimens. Often they signed their name or initials and a date. These men knew style and authentic construction techniques, and the trouble has come only after their work passed through several hands. By then the record of origin is lost, and names and dates have sometimes mysteriously disappeared. It is the work of these craftsmen that has produced the well-known "gray area" in armor collecting. Most pieces are either obviously good or obviously bad, but there is still a significant number that make collectors and curators alike feel insecure.

One type of fakery you very often encounter in armor, as well as in edged weapons, is the "upgrading" of a simple piece by the addition of etched or chiseled decoration. Here one must evaluate the work primarily by style and by patination. Usually a faker will buff a piece smooth and remove all oxidation before he begins his work. If he doesn't, the attempt at deception becomes obvious if you apply the guides discussed at the beginning of the chapter. Conversely, signs of old rust that formed after the piece was decorated are very encouraging. Usually, however, it is in the matter of style that a faker gives himself away. It is almost impossible to mimic the style of another period successfully unless the forger copies directly from an original piece. Even then, he must be very skillful to achieve the proper feeling. Most fakers tend to err badly in both style and technique. The rendition of a knight or a lady done in the Victorian period looks quite different from one done in the 16th century. So do such things as traceries or floral sprays.

Fakes in swords follow a somewhat different pattern from those of armor. Among products supposed to represent early specimens, the use of cast iron for guards and pommels is an immediate sign of recent manufacture. These elements were always forged if made of iron or steel and the decorations, if any, chiseled, etched, engraved or stamped, never cast. Often elements of two or three different swords have been combined to produce a composite specimen. Here you should be guided by style and a comparison of patination on the various elements. Also it is always wise to look at the rivet of the blade tang at the top of the pommel. Is it smooth and professional? Is it patinated in the same manner as the top of the pommel? Is there undisturbed oxidation or dirt in the narrow joint around it? Sometimes genuine old swords are taken apart to clean or to replace missing grips or grip wrappings, but the sign of a new rivet is a warning that the piece should be checked extra carefully to see if all elements match, and if there is any sign of a blade of a different size having once been used with the guard. If a wider blade had been used previously, you can usually see an area on the guard that was covered by the earlier blade and so protected from oxidation. If the piece has been taken apart once in recent years, there is no harm in doing it again so

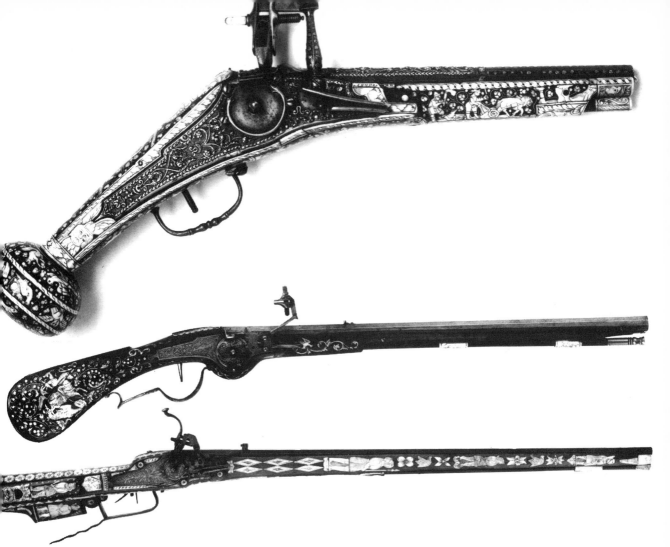

Figure 118 (top)

A wheel lock pistol assembled and decorated in the mid 19th century probably by Frédéric Spitzer. The barrel dates about 1620. It is encrusted with silver and has been shortened to fit the stock which was made about 1570 and is much more crudely decorated. The lock was assembled from odd parts in the 19th century and encrusted with silver in high relief in a way that no original wheel locks were decorated. This is typical of the "improved" firearms produced for wealthy collectors in the middle of the last century. It was owned successively by the Compte de Nieuwerkerke and Sir Richard Wallace. *Reproduced by permission of the Trustees of the Wallace Collection, London.*

Figure 119 (center)

Simple wheel lock carbine of the early 17th century that has been "upgraded" by the addition of stock inlay and etched decoration on the lock in typical Victorian style. The lock of the gun was made in the 19th century, but the rest of the carbine is genuine. *From the Study Collection of the George F. Harding Museum.*

Figure 120

Crudely constructed and decorated wheel lock rifle. The entire piece is probably late 19th or early 20th century, and the bone inlays in the stock are unbelievably bad. Yet the George F. Harding Museum has managed to acquire two very similar pieces for its Study Collection. *Courtesy the George F. Harding Museum.*

Figure 121 (top)
Detail of the second fake wheel lock in the Study Collection of the George F. Harding Museum. *Courtesy the George F. Harding Museum.*

Figure 122
The faked name "J. PHIPS" which appears on a musket assembled from various pieces. James Phips was a gunmaker in what is now Maine in the mid 17th century. Aside from the other problems with this gun, the lettering is not in the correct style for 1650. *Courtesy the Smithsonian Institution.*

you can check to see if the tang has been lengthened or ground down or altered in any other way to make it fit.

For the American market, most forgeries in recent years have involved the assembling of blades and hilts and the addition of marks and dates to make the pieces appear to be either of the Revolutionary War period or Confederate. Sometimes entire new hilts have been cast with the letters "C. S. A." or some similar Confederate device, but often the marks have just been stamped or etched on unsigned blades. These can be detected on the evidence of style faults or by the same criteria you would apply in spotting added signatures on any metal specimen.

In the firearms field, the early fakes dating from the second half of the last century primarily involved highly decorated specimens. The Paris art dealer Frédéric Spitzer employed a number of highly skilled engravers, etchers and iron chiselers who decorated plain specimens for such wealthy clients as the Rothschilds and Sir Richard Wallace. Their workmanship was often superb, but frequently they mis-dated a firearm and applied the decoration of a later period. Also they sometimes chiseled the barrels so deeply that they would have been unsafe to fire. Another functional matter that they overlooked was the fact that the lock plate of a 16th century wheel lock was normally finished flat. Etched or engraved decorations and damascening were light. The plates were never encrusted or chiseled in high relief, but Spitzer's artisans often did both. Another less skillful faker assembled a large number of wheel lock pistols from parts, making entirely new stocks. In order to save effort, he removed parts of the interior lock mechanism so that the lock mortise would be easier to cut. Apparently he was confident that his customers would not bother to remove the lock and look.

Actually, removing the lock is one of the first things you should do once a firearm has passed the first visual tests for style and decoration. When the lock has been removed you can see if it is complete, and you can see if the mortise has been altered in any way, a sure sign that the lock is not the original one. Also you can get an unobstructed view of the touch hole area. Many flint-lock arms were converted to percussion to modernize them. In recent years it has been a common practice to reconvert them to flint. This involves welding up the larger hole left by the cone seat of the percussion system and redrilling the touch hole. Normally this will be visible as an area with a distinctly different patination and surface texture from the rest of the barrel. You can detect this without removing the lock, but on cleverly done reconversions you get a better view with the lock off. In such reconversions it is necessary to replace all the external parts of the lock as well. Sometimes old parts are used; sometimes they have to be made new. On rare pieces, such as colonial weapons or Kentucky rifles, most collectors will accept a reconversion as a legitimate repair, but a reconversion is of less value than a firearm in its original condition, so you should be aware of the change.

Refinishing a firearm is another all too common practice which lessens its value. To do a good job of rebrowning or rebluing, it is necessary to buff the metal parts smooth, and this results in rounded angles on an octagonal barrel or the blurring of moldings and marks. If a piece has a fine finish but blurred and rounded angles and marks that have almost disappeared, it has obviously been refinished. Avoid it. In some instances there are small pitted areas that are so deep they cannot be removed without taking off much metal so the refinisher blues over them. There should never be any bluing or browning in a pitted area. Nor should there be finish in the recesses of marks.

Some few firearms such as Paterson and Walker Colt revolvers and Confederate revolvers have been made completely from scratch or altered from other less expensive pistols because of their great value, but most fakes in firearms made in the 18th century or later have involved simpler alterations. Standard Colt single-action revolvers have had extra pieces of barrel welded on to make them look like the long-barreled "Buntline" variation which is rare and expensive. Usually you can see the weld line if you look carefully. If you cannot detect it on the exterior of the barrel, look on the interior of the bore. If not obvious, check the serial numbers. Buntlines were made in a short range of numbers which are listed in most standard books about Colt firearms. Also, if you send the Colt Company the number, for a small fee, they will tell you what barrel length the piece was originally made in, if it had unusual features, and often who bought it. Incidentally, all the serial numbers on a Colt should match. If they don't, the piece has been assembled from odd parts. Another very simple alteration that can make a poor pistol or shoulder arm appear to be valuable is to stud it with brass-headed tacks and wrap some rawhide around it to suggest that it was used by an American Indian. This form of deception is hard to detect, but there should be dirt and corrosion under the tack heads, and the rawhide should be truly old.

The most common type of fakery, however, involves the adding of famous names—either makers or owners, or sometimes the name of an historic ship. The most spectacular of this sort of forgery involves obliterating British marks on a pocket or duelling pistol and replacing it with the name of an American maker. Some skillful fakers try to hide the evidence of the lost metal caused when grinding out the original marks by inlaying a gold plate to bear the new name. American makers seldom ever did this, in fact, and if they did, it was only on the highest quality pistols. An instance of this form of fakery and its results will be described in the last chapter. Grinding out engraved marks entails the removal of less metal than stamped marks, but even then you can usually detect the activity through changes in patination, the accidental removal of parts of original engraved decoration or follow lines around the border of a lockplate. The new marks normally give themselves away also by stylistic errors, by interrupting the patination or by the cleanness of their cuts when examined under magnification.

In short, in metal antiques, a familiarity with styles, working techniques plus an understanding of the ways in which metals oxidize are the best aids in detecting the spurious. Add to this a knowledge of the ways in which alterations can effect these factors, an awareness of the more common deceptive practices and a little common sense, and you will be protected from all but the most ingenious of forgeries.

Figure 123 (above left)
English wine glass of lead glass with a new foot made of soda glass
glued on by epoxy. Aside from the fact that the foot is incorrect in
shape and shows no signs of wear, it fluoresced yellow under ultra-
violet light while the stem and bowl fluoresced blue.

Figure 124 (above right)
Recent reproduction of a blown wine glass. The lack of signs of wear
plus the presence of vastly too many bubbles indicate the fraud.

Figure 125
The oenochoe (wine serving vessel) on the left dates from 6th-3rd
century B.C. It was made with a cored technique of molding. The
vessel on the right is a fake, probably made in Spain about 1880–1890,
and was blown in a mold. *Courtesy the Corning Museum of Glass,
Corning, N.Y.*

Figure 126 (top left)
Two engraved Stiegel-type tumblers. The left specimen was blown in a mold by the Pairpoint Corporation of New Bedford, Mass., about 1922–1930. It has a "waffle" pontil mark and is heavier than the 18th century Stiegel-type tumbler at right. Note also the differences in the engraving, especially the diamond cross-hatching. *Courtesy the Corning Museum of Glass, Corning, N.Y.*

Figure 127 (top right)
Bottom of an early 18th century wine bottle showing the pontil mark in the center and the scratches from wear around the rim.

Figure 128 (bottom left)
English 17th century glass flute, probably by George Ravenscroft. It suffers from the decomposition of the metal known as "crizzling." *Courtesy the Corning Museum of Glass, Corning, N.Y.*

Figure 129
Bottom of an early 18th century wine bottle showing the iridescent surface patination caused by a decomposition of the metal and the roughened surface around the rim where the patination has flaked off.

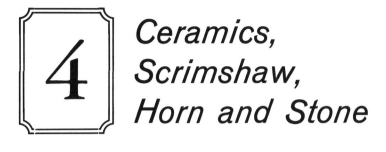

4 Ceramics, Scrimshaw, Horn and Stone

Unlike objects made of wood or metal, those made of ceramic materials, ivory, horn or stone show fewer obvious signs of age. They do not shrink. Often they do not patinate. It is fortunate that they frequently show evidence of wear and of the technique of manufacture, and that this evidence is very difficult or even impossible to reproduce. Still, the connoisseur in any of these fields must depend more heavily on a knowledge of style, color and the weight and appearance of the materials of which the genuine specimens were made.

GLASS

This is especially true in the field of glass. Reproductions have been made for centuries, but the last fifty years have seen a tremendous increase in the quantity and variety of these copies. Most have been made honestly for sale in gift shops as inexpensive decorations. Some are expensive reproductions of famous pieces and sold by museum shops; and some, of course, have been designed as frauds from the very beginning. As the years go by and the objects pass from owner to owner the distinctions blur, and gift store bottles and pitchers end up in antique shops masquerading as the real thing. Thus it is a good idea to keep abreast of the

stock displayed in gift shops and offered through mail-order cata-
logs.

The great bulk of inexpensive glass reproductions as well as
crafty fakes come from Central Europe, especially Czechoslovakia,
and from Mexico, but there is a sizable quantity also being manufactured in the United States. In almost every case the mass-pro-
duced items fail to match the originals in color, in thickness,
weight and quality of metal. Sometimes manufacturers even produce pieces in colors never used for the genuine object they simulate, and when they do attempt to copy a specific color, they are
seldom successful. The only way to prepare yourself to judge such
things as color, weight and quality of metal is to study as many
original specimens as you can, and—if you can find a nerveless
collector—pick them up so you can learn the feel. Actually, once
you have mastered the subject of color you can immediately reject
the bulk of the modern copies from halfway across a room and
dispense with a close inspection. It is essential, however, that you
look at the glass in good light. Never, never buy a piece of glass
in a dimly lit room. Beware also of one that is covered with dirt
and dust. Poor visibility can obscure more than color. It can also
hide all the other signs of authenticity that you need to assess except for general contour.

These additional clues include the quality of the metal, the very
important signs of wear and sometimes the method of manufacture. You should know whether the type of glass you are examining was originally made of soda glass, whether it had a flux
of potash which should impart a greenish tinge, if it was of lead
or "flint" glass of crystal clarity or whether accidentally or on
purpose other chemicals were added that produced variations in
color. It takes a skilled eye to detect the difference between lead
glass and the later highly refined soda-lime variety, but the difference can be seen by anyone who uses an ultra-violet light. Lead
glass will fluoresce in tints of blue, soda glass in yellow. This view-
ing technique is especially helpful in detecting modern replace-

ments of missing parts on old pieces. I own an 18th-century English wine glass (Figure 123). When examined under ultra-violet light it revealed a blue bowl and stem, a yellow foot, and an opaque white disc in between where a skillful craftsman had glued the two pieces together with epoxy. Needless to say, all parts of a glass object should be made of the same metal, and they would have been "welded" together in a hot state. The presence of epoxy or any other adhesive is at least a sign of a repair if not of a replacement.

Other signs of a metal's quality involve the presence of tiny dark flecks or air bubbles. The dark flecks result from impurities. They are frequently found in truly old specimens, but almost never in modern reproductions. Air bubbles occur in most old glass. Generally speaking, however, the better the glass the fewer and smaller the bubbles, and every glass manufacturer tried to keep them to a minimum. Here the overenthusiastic faker often betrays himself. Knowing that air bubbles appear in old glass he makes sure that his product has them, too—and he usually includes far too many of them. Mexican blown glass reproductions are especially noted for the number of their air bubbles, but any glass object loaded with bubbles except common blown bottles should be immediately suspect.

It is axiomatic that you should know how a piece in which you are interested was originally made. Was it free blown, mold blown, mold blown and expanded, or pressed? Were its decorations applied, molded, cut, engraved, etched, enamelled or cold painted? Generally speaking, a blown specimen will have a pontil mark on the bottom or a smooth depressed area where this has been ground off. Pontil marks, however, have sometimes been faked, either by applying a rough piece of glass—which you can detect if you look closely—or by molding it as part of the piece. In the latter case its contours will be much smoother than a genuine pontil mark which is almost always rough since it was produced by breaking the pontil rod free from the piece of glass it held. An object that has been blown in a mold and then expanded will always have softer contours than one that has been blown in a mold and left the same size. A specimen blown in a mold will normally have slight indentations on the inside corresponding to the raised portions on the outside. One that has been pressed will have a smooth interior unless the plunger has been incised with a design also. Normally the easiest way to detect a molded piece is to look for the mold seams. Sometimes these are cleverly concealed in the design and you have to examine the piece closely indeed—another reason for demanding good light.

When it comes to decoration there are also a few general guides that may prove useful. Cut glass is normally thicker than pressed glass, and the edges of the cuts are crisp and sharp while pressed decorations have softer edges. Sometimes a faker will dress up a pressed piece by sharpening the edges with a grinder. Usually he avoids the areas that are hard to reach, however, and so his nefarious activities are quickly identifiable. Applied decorations will have areas of undercutting which are impossible to reproduce in a mold. If engraved decoration follows proper period style, which is unusual, one must then look for signs of wear. Matte areas that have been handled frequently will not be uniformly matte and dull. Some portions will be a trifle more polished than others from the slight abrasive action of palms and fingers. It may seem strange that glass can be worn away by something as soft as a human hand, but matte areas are very delicate. Plain English wine glasses of the early to mid-18th century have frequently been "improved" by the addition of Jacobite devices or mottos because of the great demand for objects connected with the followers of the Old and Young Pretenders, and so collectors of such glasses anxiously scan the matte areas of any such glass to see if they do indeed vary in brilliance and if there are any scratches that pass into them from clear areas and so must have occurred after the engraving was done.

Enamelled decorations are seldom faked because of the extra

trouble and the dangers of damage involved in the second heating to bake the enamel. Some fakers, however, reproduce designs that should have been enamelled in cold paint; and sometimes damaged enamelled and originally cold-painted decorations have been restored with cold paint. You can usually see the difference between cold paint and enamel with nothing more than the naked eye, but in-painted areas on original cold painted decorations are more difficult when they have been skillfully done. Here, again, the ultra-violet light becomes a useful tool. It will clearly show a difference in fluorescence between the old and new paint. If the entire design has been newly painted, you must rely on style and signs of wear and damage to detect it—there will be no difference for the ultra-violet light to bring out.

While discussing decoration on glass, it might be well to mention that marks must be viewed very carefully. Normally the signatures of artists or the mark of a maker appears in a protected area on the bottom of the object. There will be little or no wear or accidental scratches to interrupt the mark and so afford evidence of age. Such marks are usually engraved with a diamond pointed tool or etched with acid. Either technique is easy for the faker to employ. Usually the only guide that you have to authenticity is the size and style of the mark, and in most cases this requires a comparison with a known specimen. Fakers often remove marks as well as add them. The McKinley Act of 1891 requires that all newly manufactured goods imported commercially into the United States be marked with the country of origin. In glassware this is done either with a paper label which comes off easily or with an etched inscription. Etched marks of this sort are always very lightly done, and so a dishonest person can quickly polish them out. Because the amount of grinding required is minimal, it is difficult if not impossible to see. In rare instances pressed glass has the country of origin indented in the mold so that it appears in raised letters. Such labels are difficult to obliterate, but I have seen one or two instances where someone has attempted it.

When a glass object passes all the tests of style, method of manufacture, weight, color and quality of metal, the final and crucial examination involves the signs of wear. Polish from fingers on matte areas has already been mentioned, but most wear is caused by dust. Household dust is filled with abrasive particles. These particles cut into the bottom of a piece of glass when it is moved around on a tabletop or a shelf. Heavily used specimens show almost a frosted appearance on the high spots of the bottom. When you look at these spots under even moderate magnification you will see that they are composed of a myriad of small scratches, some of them very tiny. Since each of them was produced by a different particle, each scratch will be of a different width, depth and length, and there will be no area of exactly parallel scratches. There is no way a forger can duplicate this appearance without spending thousands and thousands of hours, and even then I doubt that he could do it convincingly. Scratches will also appear on places other than the bottom. These will be isolated, individual lines, usually invisible to the naked eye. But if you go over the exterior of an old piece with just a five-power magnifier, you should find a number of them. If you don't, stop and wonder. Next to the bottom of the foot, the inside of a glass is the best place to look for scratches. If the glass has been stored in an upright position and the maid or housewife has wiped the bowl out with a dry cloth from time to time, she would be bound to cause some scratches. If the glass has been stored upside down, there should be scratches on the lip. Other obvious places to look are the areas of widest diameter where an object would be apt to strike another object set next to it in a closet, then the sides of a spout or handle, and so on. But scratches can and do show up almost any place. The location of their appearance should cause little wonder; only their absence is reason to worry.

Glass can show evidences of age in ways other than wear. One is through the decomposition of the alkaline content of the metal. George Ravenscroft, who introduced the manufacture of lead glass

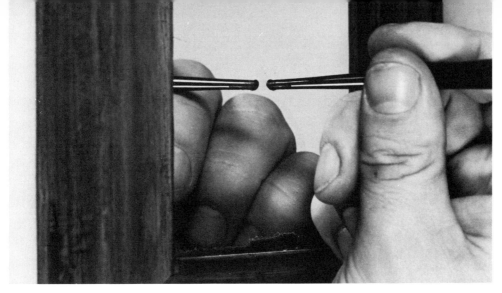

Figure 130 (top)
Method of measuring the thickness of a mirror in an early 18th century frame. In this instance the thickness is so great that it indicates a modern replacement immediately even without checking for other evidences of age.

Figure 131
Portion of an Adam style mirror showing the loss of refraction caused by the breakdown of the mirror backing.

in England in the 17th century, had difficulty with this. Many of his pieces developed opaque white lines and areas with a slight roughening of the surface. At first glance this looks somewhat like mineral deposits left on the surface from the evaporation of hard water. Actually it is a deterioration of the glass itself. Collectors call this type of decomposition "crizzling." Decomposition of a very similar sort can also be seen in later glass from England, the United States and northern Europe. Glass that has been buried for long periods of time also alters in appearance, again largely through changes in the alkaline content. Excavated Roman glass is noted for its iridescent patina and the scaly nature of its surface, but the most striking examples of this deterioration are often found in bottles recovered from seawater. In all instances the surface of the glass has actually deteriorated and lost some or all of its translucence. This scale will usually flake off and reveal a rough surface beneath, but sometimes the deterioration has continued all the way through.

Glass exposed to sunlight will also change in color. Depending upon the original color of the glass it may turn violet, yellow, greenish or just to a darker shade of its original hue. Again this is usually the result of changes in the alkaline content. Normally it takes at least ten years of exposure to bright sunlight to produce a visible change in color. There are some collectors who specialize in these color differences and collect the violet-hued bottles found in ghost towns of the American West. To the best of my knowledge no one as yet has tried to fake these color and surface alterations.

WINDOW GLASS AND MIRRORS

It makes considerable difference in the value of a breakfront, corner cupboard or mirror if the glass is original or at least replaced with other glass of the proper type. Thus you, as a collector, should know how to recognize old panes of glass whether or not they have been backed with silver to make them reflective. There are three principal ways of making the sheet glass with which you should be familiar.

The earliest method produced crown or "bull's eye" glass. To make it a glassblower took from the furnace a large gather of molten glass on the end of his blow-iron. He then blew and marvered the gather until he had produced a large hollow globe. At this point, an assistant attached an iron pontil rod opposite the blow-iron which was then broken away. Breaking off the blow-iron left a hole in the globe, and the glassworker could then spin the rod until the globe flattened out into a thin disc. After this had been accomplished the pontil was cut free with shears leaving a bump and shear marks that produced the characteristic "bull's eye." All of this required frequent reheating and annealing and often involved as many as ten different laborers. When the annealed sheet had cooled, it was cut into panes of the desired size and shape. The "bull's eye" itself was usually set aside for remelting, but sometimes a pane including it would be used for a small window where light but not visibility was important—or for a lantern. It would never have been used for a piece of quality furniture or for an important window. Sheet glass made by the crown method can be recognized by the slightly arced striations or ripples in the surface or by the way air bubbles when present seem to follow an arc. The sizes of sheets made by this method were severely restricted if one eliminated the center, and by 1830 it was obsolete to all intents and purposes.

The second method was the hand-cylinder process. In this the blower and his assistants formed the gather of glass into a long cylinder, cut off the ends, slit it down the center and flattened it out into a sheet. This method allowed the production of larger sheets than the crown process, and there was no need to eliminate the "bull's eye" in the center. The entire sheet could be used as one piece if desired. This manufacturing technique was well estab-

lished in eastern France and the German states very early in the
1800's. Lucas Chance carried it to England in 1832, and it probably
reached America at least that early. Cylinder blown glass can be
recognized by the fact that such striations and air bubbles as may
be found follow a generally straight line instead of an arc.

At the same time that crown and cylinder glass were being
made, a completely different manufacturing technique for sheets
was also employed. This was the casting of plate glass. As early as
1688 the King of France granted a monopoly to one company for
the production of cast plate glass, and by 1760 its output was 1,000
tons a year. An attempt to cast plate glass was made in England as
early as 1691, but it was not successfully accomplished until the
1770's. America imported sheet glass from Britain and Europe
until well into the 19th century. The process of casting sheet glass
consisted of pouring the molten glass onto a metal table with
raised edges and rolling it flat under heavy pressure. After it had
cooled it was reheated for annealing and then polished smooth.

All forms of sheet glass were smoothed and polished. As a rule,
the better quality they were, the more smoothly they were polished, but they were never quite as smooth as later glass. Also,
early sheets were normally much thinner. In order to judge the
thickness of a mirror, you have only to place the point of a pencil
or pen against the surface and note the distance between the point
and its image which is actually reflected on the silver at the back
of the sheet. Mirrors offer several other clues besides thickness in
assessing their age. There is a different, darker reflective quality in
most mirrors made before the mid-19th century. It is impossible
to describe, but you will become aware of it if you examine a
quantity of genuine specimens. Also the backing frequently has
broken down in one or more areas so that there are non-reflective
spots. If you can see the back of the mirror, you have further
guides. The earliest mirrors were usually backed with tin foil
and mercury which was then painted with a thick black paint or
red lead. By the mid-19th century most makers had begun to use

Figure 132 (above left)
Delft inkstand. The drawer, inserted pen holder at left on the top, and the head of the figure have been newly made and replaced. Note the difference in the decorative designs. The modern pieces have blurred edges on the decorations whereas the originals are crisp.

Figure 133 (above right)
Plate and cup of Chinese export porcelain. Note that the gold blindfold on the figure of justice on the cup and the gold decorations in the panel have almost completely worn away. The gold decorations are the first to wear off porcelain of this type.

Figure 134 (bottom left)
Red earthenware dish with slip decoration. Note the scratches and areas where the glaze has worn off. These are good signs of age and use and do not damage the desirability of the piece from the collector's standpoint.

Figure 135
A pearlware plate (left) and a creamware plate (right) excavated from a trash pit at Plymouth, Mass. Note the knife scratches which are especially visible on the pearlware. These specimens have been damaged so severely that they have lost their market value for most collectors, but they do show some of the signs of use that one should look for. *Courtesy Plimoth Plantation.*

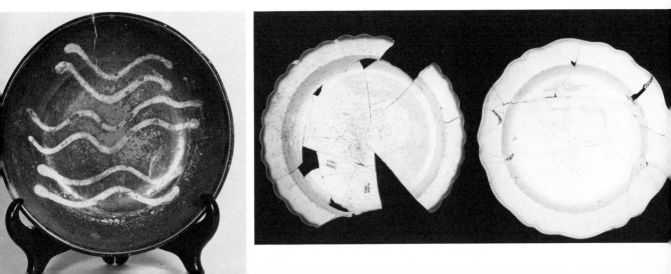

Figure 136 (top)
Liverpool pitcher of about 1800 with replaced handle of incorrect form.

Figure 137
Detail of the Liverpool pitcher in the previous illustration. Note the crudeness of the modeling and the difference between its finish and the crackled glaze of the pitcher body.

a silver solution with a precipitating agent that deposited a pebbly coating of silver on the glass. Still, they usually added a coat of black paint. Modern mirrors are spray coated, often with aluminum, with a backing of red paint. When you look at the back of a mirror, however, you should remember that over the years many people have preferred visibility to authenticity and so have had their mirrors resilvered. Thus the glass itself is the only real clue to age. The backing can confirm its antiquity, but it cannot disprove it.

One final comment about sheet glass. If you can look at the cut or broken edge of a sheet and detect a yellowish or yellow-brown color it indicates the presence of selenium and a probable date of 1900 or later.

POTTERY AND PORCELAIN

Pottery and porcelain objects have been made for so many years, in so many cultures and in such a multitude of types that it is impossible to describe all the signs of falsification in any short essay. It would require a book in itself and probably no one person would be qualified to write it. Generally speaking, however, the detection of a fake depends upon aberrations in manufacture, style and materials—as in any other field. Be sure you know the material—whether earthenware, stoneware, true porcelain or soft porcelain—that the original was made in, the type of glaze and the style and method of decoration that should be found in the type of piece you are considering. There have been some excellent forgeries of Sèvres and Delft and some Etruscan and Oriental wares that are difficult even for the expert to sort out, but most fakes fail badly in one or more of these areas. Once you are thoroughly familiar with the materials, method of manufacture and style of decoration, you can protect yourself adequately. A piece that has been decorated in paint instead of slip—as in the case of some spurious Greek vases, and even American redware—

is easy to detect. Modern Delft reproductions that have printed designs rather than hand-painted ones are also easy. Viewed under magnification a printed design shows a dot-screen, especially in the mid-tone ranges, instead of a solid brush stroke. Even the recent painted Delft usually has a thicker body and darker colors than old pieces. Sometimes fakers are careless enough to decorate or place a mark over a glaze when the originals of that type were decorated before glazing.

Repairs and touched-up decorations are among the commonest hazards in the fields collected today, and this touching up frequently involves the removal, alteration or addition of marks. Because he fears sags in the original glaze and color changes in the decorations, the restorer, retoucher or mark artist almost never tries to reglaze the entire piece. Instead he will use a simulated glaze that he can paint on. This is often difficult to see with the naked eye, but sometimes it can be seen under ultra-violet light. I own an Oriental export punch bowl in the rose medallion pattern. It had had a small piece broken out at the rim, and this piece had been cleverly cemented back in place. I lived with this bowl for several years before I happened to look at it under ultra-violet light and discovered the repair. Since it was an honest repair with the original fragment it did not bother me particularly, but if I had paid a high price for a perfect specimen, I would have been less than happy with my discovery. Often you will find a spot on the bottom of a piece of porcelain or pottery where the tell-tale label of the country of origin has been removed and a small dab of simulated glaze painted on. This is a sure sign of chicanery since someone removed the evidence that the piece was made after the McKinley Act of 1891 which required this label. Sometimes you can see this with the naked eye, but ultra-violet light will more often reveal it. If the faker has thought to coat the entire bottom with his simulated glaze, there will be no difference in the fluorescence. Thus it is wise to look at the top under the light also and see if it fluoresces the same color. Seldom will the forger go to the trouble of coating the whole object.

I saw an interesting example of this recently during a seminar on fakes that I was teaching. One of my students brought in a small spatterware plate. Such ware commands relatively high prices these days, and he was curious about its authenticity. We had no genuine example to compare it with, but the design generally looked good. The bottom showed obvious signs of wear, and there was no doubt that it was indeed an old plate. Once we put the piece under ultra-violet light, however, the fraud showed up immediately. The glaze on the underside fluoresced an entirely different color from that on top. The original maker would have used the same glaze on the entire piece.

In the last few years a new formula for simulated glaze has been developed that cannot be detected under ultra-violet light when the new glaze is applied to pieces with a compatible original glaze. Oriental export porcelain is one type of ware on which this new paint glaze is especially effective. Fortunately its use is not yet widespread. The only way to circumvent the deception of this new material, which so skillfully hides a repair you are apt to miss it in a visual check, is to hold the piece up against a bright light. True porcelain is translucent, and the amount of light it lets through is normally determined by thickness or surface decoration. The cement and synthetic glaze, however, interfere with the light transmission. Thus, if you see any dark line or area that you cannot explain by variations of thickness or decoration, check the surface very carefully under a bright raking light and be very skeptical.

Signs of wear vary according to the type of porcelain and pottery. True porcelain is so hard that even an unglazed rim on the bottom will not scratch in ordinary use. Decorations applied over the glaze, however, will wear off in areas of heavy use. This is especially true of gold. Earthenware and some stoneware will scratch and chip more easily, and so you can often find evidence of use. If the effects of wear are too severe, they damage the value of the object; if minor or inconspicuous, they are a real comfort.

New Wedgwood pieces are in no way to be considered fakes or reproductions since they are still being made by the same firm. If you collect old Wedgwood, however, you would be wise to know the differences between new and old pieces. Most obvious are the jasper wares with classical decorations in white relief. The new pieces lack the definition in detail that you find in the old ones. In some of the cheaper Japanese and German reproductions the decorations are molded as integral parts of the piece instead of being added separately before firing.

Steins are another popular collecting field with numerous modern imitations being produced in Germany, Japan and England. The new ones, however, fail obviously to match the original colors, and the metal ornaments are poorly cast. This is especially true of those with military or railroad decorations as finials. Period steins with these sculptured finials have fine detail. The modern ones are fuzzy and poor, and you can usually see traces of the mold seams. Also, since steins are made of fairly soft earthenware, there are usually many signs of wear and use in the form of scratches, nicks and chips.

Lusterware, silver-resist tea sets, Toby jugs, and Staffordshire figurines have been widely reproduced in recent years. Almost all of the new pieces, however, are thicker and heavier than the originals, details in the designs and modeling are sloppy, and the colors do not match those of authentic specimens. A quick comparison with an authentic piece or sometimes even a good picture is all that you need to recognize them.

Because ceramics are so durable, because they do not shrink and almost never patinate, there are few guides of the type available to connoisseurs in other fields. In the main you must rely on a knowledge of materials, methods of manufacture and style—and be especially alert for signs of repair and restoration.

Figure 138
Genuine mid-19th century scrimshaw engraving on whale tooth. *Courtesy E. Norman Flayderman.*

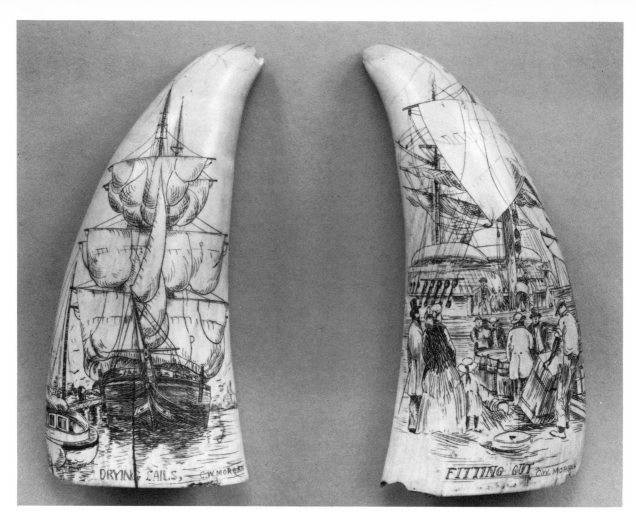

Figure 139 (above)
Two whale teeth engraved by "Perry" of New Bedford, Mass. about 1940–1950. "Perry" seems to have used the ship *Charles W. Morgan* at Mystic Seaport plus some elements from 19th century woodcuts for his inspiration, but his technique is purely 20th century. *Courtesy E. Norman Flayderman.*

Figure 140
An engraved whale tooth signed by "Frank" who is presumably still working in the New Bedford area. The engraving technique is purely modern, and the portrait of the *Charles W. Morgan* shows it in a position never seen on early scrimshaw. Still it is collectible as a piece of modern art. *Courtesy E. Norman Flayderman.*

SCRIMSHAW

Scrimshaw is a term that means many things to many people. In its widest usage it covers all the decorative and useful objects carved by sailors from whale, walrus or even elephant ivory, whalebone, baleen or wood. Almost all the faking in the scrimshaw field, however, is confined to the engraving of pictures, designs or messages on ivory or whalebone. Plain whale teeth can be purchased for a relatively small sum, and a skillful engraver can make a tidy profit—if he can find a gullible customer. It should be mentioned, however, that some modern engravers decorate whale teeth and sell them as contemporary art. As such they are legitimate, but they should not be confused with antique or semi-antique specimens.

If you are thinking of purchasing a piece of engraved scrimshaw, there are several things to watch for, and these will help you eliminate all but the very best of the forgeries. For one thing, a sailor engraving a whale tooth had more time than anything else. There was absolutely no hurry. Therefore, he normally sanded the ridges off both sides of the tooth, using sharkskin, pumice or, in later years, sandpaper to make the whole tooth smooth before he began his engraving. Thus, if you find a tooth with one grooved side and one side smoothed and engraved, look it over very very carefully. Everything else would have to be completely above suspicion before you should even consider it. Another aspect to check is the color. When engraved, the tooth was white, but ivory yellows with time, and this yellowing is very difficult to duplicate convincingly by chemical means. Heat will produce a reasonable yellow color, but it also makes the tooth very brittle. Packing a piece of ivory in damp tea leaves or manure for a few days will also produce a yellow color that approximates an age patina.

If your eye is not skilled enough to detect these false patinations, an ultra-violet light can be of considerable assistance. Ivory that has yellowed with age will normally fluoresce a mottled and dull yellow with perhaps some white areas where wear has removed some of the patina. New ivory that has been artificially stained will often fluoresce with a brownish or even a deep blue-violet color depending upon the staining agent. Ivory that has been buried in manure will fluoresce brilliantly, but the application of alcohol on a swab will remove the fluorescence. New ivory or ivory that has been cleaned with water, solvents or abrasion will fluoresce a brilliant white. A specimen that appears gleaming white either to the naked eye or under ultra-violet illumination should cause you to consider the possibility of fraud or, at the very least, over-cleaning. Bone, incidentally, will normally fluoresce a fairly clear white even when it has a legitimate yellow patina under normal light. It is impossible to describe the differences in white and yellow color variation in a way that will be of real help to you. The only way to become truly familiar with the variations one can expect in fluorescence is to experiment and compare new and old surfaces under the same ultra-violet light in the same degree of darkness.

Even more important than surface texture or color is the decoration itself. The language, spelling, style and technique of drawing should all be proper for the period. Authentic scrimshaw continued to be made into the present century so there is room for considerable variation, but each element should conform to the supposed period of the engraving. Among these, ships are perhaps the best guides. Since the engravers were sailors, they knew sailing vessels well. They would make no mistakes in form or rigging for the type of vessel intended, though they sometimes omitted details. Also, in ninety-nine cases out of a hundred, they showed the vessel in profile. Once in a great while you may find a view that portrays a stern or a portion of the stern. But if you ever see an engraving of a ship approaching you at a three quarter angle with the waves billowing from the bow, turn your back and walk rapidly away. The same criterion of authenticity should also be

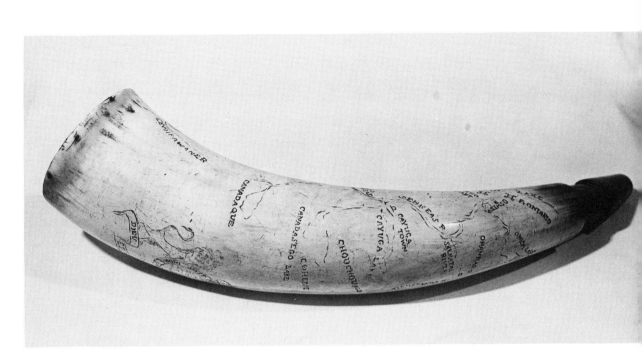

Figures 141 A & B

Two views of a recently engraved powder horn offered on the market for well over $1,000. It passed through several hands before being taken out of circulation. The faker used an old horn but then cleaned the surface. Many of the scratches were on the horn before it was engraved. The style of lettering is incorrect for period with the letters and numbers especially bad, and there are no convincing signs of wear. *Courtesy the New York State Historical Association.*

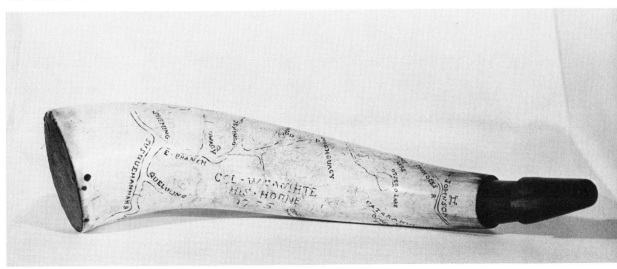

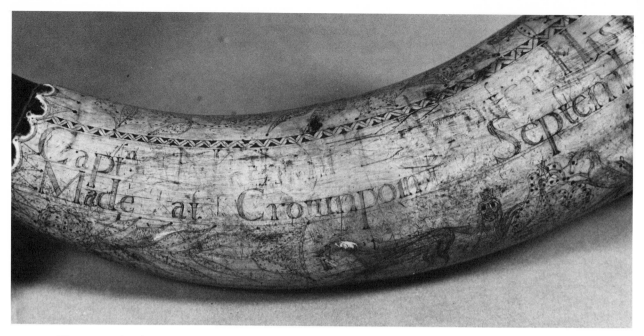

Figure 142 (top)

Portion of a powderhorn engraved in 1759. The engraving style and technique are what one would expect for the period, and, since this is the side worn next to the body, the owner's name in the top line of the inscription has almost completely worn off.

Figure 143

The butt end of the innerside of a plain 18th century powder horn. Long rubbing against the body has polished the horn to a high gloss and worn the wooden plug so that parts of the turned grooves have disappeared.

applied to any nautical gear included as ornament. Sometimes these objects, like the ships, were stylized, but they would never be unworkable. Contemporary prints often provided inspiration for the artist, and the identification of these can be helpful although a later workman could copy a period print just as well.

These guides, admittedly, are few. They are not entirely fool-proof, but you will be surprised how many fakes you can eliminate by applying them.

HORN

Engraved horn is in many ways similar to scrimshaw, and many of the same criteria apply to detecting fakes in this field, but there are other guides as well. Few engraved scrimshaw objects saw much use. Thus signs of wear are minimal, if indeed they are present. Horn objects usually were utilitarian and so you can hope for evidence of wear. Also you should check the type of horn to see if it came from the proper animal.

Horn color, like hair color, varies from breed to breed. The idea of developing and raising pure-bred stock did not become popular until the mid-19th century, and even in the early 20th century small farmers considered it of little importance. The availability of a sire was more important than his breed. Generally speaking, however, the cattle available in most of Britain and America in the 17th and 18th centuries were Durham or Devon types—if one ignores the Highland variety. Some black and white cattle are mentioned in America at least as early as the 1750's, and these may have been Dutch Belted. Holsteins begin to appear in small numbers about 1800. Thus for an early horn one would expect a gray-green or yellow color with some black areas, usually at the tip. Horns with strongly contrasting black and white areas are most likely 19th century or later. With these color factors in mind, you can look at a horn spoon, cup or powder horn and quickly decide if it is apt to be 19th century rather than earlier.

In recent years a pair of long horns, reminiscent of the longhorn cattle of the early West, have become popular bar decorations. Real longhorn trophies more than 60 years old are rare, and so the demand has been met by importing longhorns from Mexico or the horns of African cattle. Not only are these African horns usually longer than the Spanish-American longhorn originals, but again they have sharply contrasting black and white areas similar to but more obvious than the real thing. Not content with the natural length of the imported trophies, the entrepreneurs who sell them often mount them on the ends of a tooled leather roll that is a foot and a half or more long in itself!

In the horn field, the most expensive, and therefore the most frequently faked object has been the engraved powder horn, though engraving has also been added to cups and boxes as well. In judging a powder horn, you should first check to see if it came from the proper type of animal for its period. Then look to see if it has been made correctly. Are the carvings and decorative moldings at the nozzle end proper for the period? Good pieces will have been scraped with a knife or piece of glass, then polished with pumice or sand until they are smooth or even thinned to the point of translucency so that the user could judge the amount of gunpowder he had left. Often this was followed with a shellac finish. Before applying the finish, however, the maker cut the plug for the big end, softened the horn in hot water, and forced the plug in so that it fit tightly. To secure the plug he used hardwood pegs or nails. You should check these to see that they are the proper type for the period—hand forged or cut. Screws or staples for attaching the thong should be handmade. Remember, though, that plugs are sometimes replaced. A horn that has lost its plug is especially susceptible to damage, and many collectors have replaced missing plugs as a protective measure.

The real test, however, lies in the engraving. Many fakers do their work on old powder horns, and in these cases all the other tests for age are meaningless. In assessing the engraving the main

Figure 144 (top)
Medieval stone sculpture from India. Note the differing degrees of patination caused by the varying lengths of time that areas have been exposed to the atmosphere. The broken surfaces at the bottom have been exposed so long that their color matches the rest of the figure. The light gray area at the back from just above the elbow down is much more recent, probably about fifty years old, and there are a few very white areas in it that must be quite recent.

Figure 145
Obsidian points purchased recently from country people in Mexico. They are not properly flaked and were probably less than a week old when bought.

Figure 146 (above left)
Partially finished effigy in obsidian. The abraded area below the head is still rough, and the form resembles no early prototype.

Figure 147 (above right)
Fake stone objects. The shapes are poor, the flaking bad, and there is no patination. The three pieces at right are being offered by mail by their makers as "souvenirs."

Figure 148
Partially finished fake of a grooved stone axe. The maker was using a metal tool to form the groove.

criterion is style. The letters in names or inscriptions should be proper for the period. So should the style of drawing. Some very fine fake horns have been engraved in New England, New York and in Great Britain, but in every case that I have known the fakers have failed to match period styles exactly. Every period and every engraver has peculiar characteristics, and with experience, one can often begin to recognize the work of the more prolific fakers even when it is not possible to learn their true identities.

Aside from errors in style, the fakers frequently make mental errors that help you reject their handiwork. They show flags not in use at the supposed period or indicate forts or settlements either not in existence at the time or known by a different name. Sometimes they will indicate roads or the names of mountain ranges, and that was almost never done in the 18th century. And frequently they will lapse into modern idiom. One major American museum has an engraved powder horn that makes almost every possible mistake in its engraved decoration. Indians are drawn in good 19th century style. Forts and buildings are delineated in true perspective, which was never done. Firearms are drawn in realistic detail, and to top all this it bears the statement "Saw Tim Murfy plug Gen Frazer at near ¼ mile." Not only is "plug" a modern slang term, but recent research indicates it is highly unlikely that Timothy Murphy shot General Fraser, popular folklore notwithstanding. Rarely do you have the fortune to find a horn with so many errors. In most cases the mistakes are fewer, the style aberrations more subtle. And the best fakers can make life difficult indeed.

If there are no obvious errors in construction or decoration, sometimes the usual signs of age and use will help confirm or deny the authenticity of a horn. Some early horns may have been put away immediately upon completion, wrapped and stored so carefully that they never suffered the vicissitudes of time. Most horns, however, will show some of the effects of use. The rubbing of the strap around the neck of the horn will usually produce some wear, although it is often hard to see. The most obvious signs of use will be found on the side of the horn that rubbed against the wearer's body. Here the friction has frequently rubbed off the finish, dimmed or even obliterated the engraving. Then there are the nicks, scratches and occasional insect holes that develop over the years. On an engraved horn, these blemishes should always cut across the engraved lines, indicating that they came after the decoration. If an engraved line slips into the edge of a scratch or hole, it is a bad omen indeed. Few engravers would leave a blemish on a horn they intended to decorate, and certainly none would have bothered with a horn that had a hole in it.

The engraving on cups and boxes is usually simpler than that on powder horns, but the criteria for judging them are the same. Is the engraving in proper style? Are there the expected signs of wear and did they come after the decoration? Is the horn from a logical breed or species? Only when you can answer all these question with a definite "yes" should you feel comfortable with the piece of horn you are examining.

STONE

To many, stone is a permanent, unchanging material. In reality it is anything but. It erodes, it breaks, it stains and it patinates. Only if it is protected from the elements and left untouched by human hands will its surface remain stable. And even then, the outside will gradually acquire a patina that gives it a slightly different color from the one it bore when first cut. Statues, relief ornaments and column capitals exposed to the sulphur laden air of modern cities rapidly erode and patinate, but even sandstone sculpture from non-industrial areas of India often show signs of erosion and color change.

Sculptural ornaments have been faked for centuries. Michelangelo carved a false Roman cupid to deceive a high official of the church. Such early forgeries, like the later neo-classical creations of the 18th century, are desirable antiques in their own right, and they have every sign of age that you could wish because they are indeed old. In such cases you can only use style and technique as guides. To weed out newer reproductions, however, you can look for cracks and chips which reveal a difference in color plus a softening of outline and detail from the action of rain, dust and chemicals in the air. Using these criteria you can quickly recognize the sculptures broken or sawed from their original mountings by recent archeological thieves, for the cut portion will be radically different in color and very fresh looking. The desecrations of these pillagers are deplorable, but if you get the chance to study a few of the pieces they have smuggled from their native lands you can get a clear understanding of the ways in which outdoor stonework alters in appearance over the years. Some artificial staining with chemicals has been done by clever forgers, especially on marble. Occasionally they have been very successful, but more often they produce unusual colors and unexplainable blotches.

The most commonly faked stone objects are the simple paleolithic and neolithic tools, weapons and ornaments of Europe and of the American Indian. As long ago as 1841 a Yorkshireman named Edward Simpson produced hundreds of "ancient" stone artifacts. Known familiarly as "Flint Jack" or "Fossil Willy" to the antiquarians of his day, he successfully sold his work as genuine despite the fact that his designs were remarkably original. To this day others have followed in his footsteps. The country people of Mexico, in fact, derive a good income from the production of obsidian points and effigies which they offer at local markets complete with tales of their discovery while tilling the fields. Chipping flint, quartz, or chert is actually a very simple operation, and I once watched an experienced flint craftsman produce a very passable quartz arrowhead in a few minutes. Then he made another from the bottom of a Coca-Cola bottle!

There are a few stone craftsmen who know the archeological

field well enough to produce fakes that are stylistically correct. Most, however, make mistakes either in the method of flaking or grinding or in the size and form of the object. Unusual shapes, of course, attract the gullible collector who hopes he has discovered a great rarity. Even professional archeologists who scorn artifacts without provenance have occasionally been gulled by pranksters who "planted" spurious pieces during an excavation. In general, whenever you encounter any prehistoric or ethnological stone artifact that strays from the norm in shape or size you should regard it with considerable skepticism.

Probably the commonest of all fakes of simple stone artifacts are original specimens that have been reworked. A craftsman of easy conscience may find a broken spearpoint or a simple blade and decide to convert it into a more desirable or at least a seemingly complete specimen. Here is where a knowledge of patination and weathering is essential. As mentioned above, stone does indeed patinate and change color. It even picks up mineral deposits. New flaking should be apparent because it will almost always interfere with the original pattern of flakes. Also it will reveal a clean surface of a different color from the untouched portions of the piece. The type and color of the patination will vary depending upon the age of the piece, the type of stone and the soil and area in which it has been found. But there will always be a color change, and usually it will be greater on one side than another. Unless the artifact has come from a cave or some other protected place, there will also be a burnishing or softening of the surface. Scars from new flaking are sharp. Old ones are normally much softer.

These are the general principles to bear in mind. Different varieties of stone, different climatic conditions, and the degree of protection from the elements will all affect the nature and extent of the evidence of age. The main thing is to be sure you understand the clues and can logically explain the variances. This plus a knowledge of styles and of working techniques are your best protections against being fooled.

Figure 149
One of a pair of British pistols that
have been increased in value by the addition of an American maker's marks.
Despite this alteration the pistols were
held legally genuine by a British court.
Courtesy National Park Service.

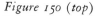

Figure 150 (top)
Detail of the lockplate of the pistol. Note how the area in front of the cock has been filed down to remove the original maker's name. This has roughened the surface and obliterated the engraved followline that runs along the bottom edge of the lockplate from the rear before it disappears below the inlaid gold plate with the fictitious maker's mark. It picks up again just under the finial of the frizzen spring at the far right and continues all around the lock. The engraved decoration above the new mark has also been disturbed. *Courtesy National Park Service.*

Figure 151
Portion of a page from a recent catalog offering a collection of fake Colt revolvers—as fakes—along with documentation—for $2,750.00 *Courtesy E. Norman Flayderman.*

*1166A.

THE GREAT AMERICAN GUN HOAX OF ALL TIME. HERE THEY ARE IN ALL THEIR GLORY OR INFAMY--HOWEVER YOU CHOOSE TO CALL IT. Four famed so-called "COLT-WALKER-COLLINS" Colts or "EDGERLY" Colts or the "PATERSON-WALKER" Colts. These guns have quite a history that goes way back to the early 1930's. They were sold during that period for approximately $6000 (when the best Walker Colt never brought $1000) & which would be the equivalent of $75,000 sale or more on the current market! Remember, those were depression days too.) They first appeared in the famous & much respected Theodore Dexter's "Antique Weapon Trade Journal" of January 1931 & are shown on the cover of that catalog which presented the famed McMurdo Silver collection of Colts with the first 2pp completely devoted to the importance of these four pieces. They next appeared in the Theodore Dexter list of April 1937 in a series of 7 photographs with full descriptions of each & a Dexter "Certificate of Authenticity" verifying their originality & appraising them as of December 1936 at $15,000 current market value!! In 1937 there then appeared a special booklet of 26pp called "The Revolving Cylinder Colt Pistol Story 1839-1847" by James Edgerly completely devoted to these four guns & their importance as bridging the Colt gap between the Paterson & the Walker Model 1839-1847. Not only authenticating them for the collecting world, but showing their great importance as unique variants of Colts (2 of them actually bear the Paterson, N.J. address!). All 4 guns are given exceptional credence & authenticity by one of the most well known of antique arms collectors & gun authors, Claud Fuller, & they appear (Plate 18) & are thoroughly discussed as orig in his classic work "WHITNEY FIREARMS" Pub. 1946. Next we come to the Feb. 1959 issue of GUN REPORT where all 4 of these guns again appear in an article "FIVE RARE COLTS" (they are shown with 1 real Colt Walker) furthering their claims to fame; a final note being in the March 1959 issue (buried in the back pages) retracting the credence of the previous Gun Report story & mentioning "Accurate & unimpeachable information available to us states that these 4 guns were made by a gunsmith in Colorado in 1920...the guns have over the years gained notoriety because of complicated story associated with them, etc." which of course is the accurate & truth about the whole matter! Photostatic copies of all this mentioned material & background will go with the 4 guns as well as an orig copy of the Edgerly booklet. All 4 are Walker size & larger (2 of them being 25% larger than the Walker!). Impractical to give entire itemized details of each here, but briefly they are: (1) Huge "Paterson-Walker" allegedly the first attempt by Colt in 1837-8 to fabricate the Walker while still in N,J,! Massive 19" overall piece with 10" bbl actually mkd "Patent Arms Mfg. Co. , Paterson, N.J. -Colt's Patent." Weighs 6½ lbs. Made without lever or provision for same. (2) Also massive perc revolver 17" overall with 9½" bbl mkd "Address Col. Colt-London" with a unique loading lever design & operation & representing the addition of Captain Walker's loading lever ideas with a real gobble-de-gook dissertation on why it is mkd London! This piece weighs 6½ lbs too. (3) The so-called "Perfected" 1840 Walker Colt revol; just about standard Walker size. Quite finely made & mkd in early script-like letters similar to those on all Patersons "Patent Arms Mfg Co. -Paterson, N.J. -Colt's Patent." This supposedly to quote "The Walker Model that was ready for production" when Colt was double crossed by his Paterson's executive & forced to tie up the Paterson Armory" & a piece that resulted from a compromise between Walker & one T. Collins who plays an important role in this affair. It is quite fine condition with most orig blue, just wearing thin & fading with casehard too & quite well looks the part. (4) Another piece almost identical to the above Walker. Different finish; showing wear & use & aging; mkd "Address Col. Colt-London." Differences in the notch on bbl lug for loading; this allegedly being the Walker that Colt intended for exhibit to an English Ordnance Board. Condition is interesting in that they all do have quite an appearance of authenticity & age. Remember each of these completely hand crafted from beginning to end. Aging different, one being very fine, another being age brown, patches light pitting--so that they all do look different. All work perfect mechanically. Actually a fantastic amount of effort & work went into the preparation & mfr of these pieces & they did leave a rather regrettable trail of carnage & tears behind them not to mention a few blemished reputations. They do represent a most intriguing facet of gun collecting history. They are very fairly & moderately priced for all four pieces with their supporting documentation .2750.00

5 *When You Have Bought a Fake*

Every collector has had the experience. Through carelessness or lack of knowledge he has bought a piece that is not what he thought it was. Sometimes he discovers his error himself. Sometimes a friend gleefully points it out. No matter how it occurs, it can be a shattering experience, and it raises the inevitable question: What do I do now? Do I "bite the bullet" and take the loss or can I get my money back? The answer depends on two things —the circumstances under which you bought the fake and your conscience.

If you bought the piece from a reputable dealer, the chances are good he will take it back. Many of the better dealers will guarantee to take back any piece they sell no matter what the reason and apply the purchase price against another item in their shop. They normally do not make cash refunds because of the paperwork and tax complications involved or because of a possible shortage of fluid capital. Still, with dealers who subscribe to this practice you are guaranteed that you will not be stuck with a piece you have come to suspect. It is a good idea, especially for beginners, to discuss this subject with the dealer before buying.

Some dealers may be reluctant to guarantee the right of exchange. In such cases there is the option of requesting a bill of sale that states categorically that the object purchased is of the period represented and notes any repairs or restorations. With such a document you have the basis for a suit for fraud if the object turns out to be a fake, but such action is not always foolproof. You have to be able to prove that the piece is a fake or otherwise not as represented. This is not always easy, especially if the trial judge is not familiar with antiques. American courts have held that a dealer selling an antique has qualified himself as an expert, which helps somewhat, but British courts take a slightly different view.

Let me give you one example of the hazards of a suit for fraud in a British court. A friend of mine purchased a pair of English flintlock pistols from a British dealer. They bore the name of an American maker whose works command a high price, and he was delighted to get them. Friends quickly pointed out that the pistols were British in style, that the stocks were English walnut, not American black walnut. They laid a straight-edge along the top of the barrel, revealing a scooped out area where something, presumably a mark, had been ground off, and they pointed out that there had been filing on the lockplate that destroyed part of the ornamental engraving while the American maker's name in a gold inlay appeared across this area in crisp letters. Faced with this evidence, my friend asked for a refund or exchange, was refused, and brought suit. At the trial, experts from leading museums pointed out the worrisome evidence and testified that they considered the American marks to be entirely false. They could not convince the judge, and he declared the pistols genuine. The verdict was appealed, but there had been no incorrect procedures so the appeal failed. My friend was thus stuck with pistols that were legally genuine, but no collector would touch them after the publicity of the trial even if he had wanted to pass them off. With the legal costs added to the original purchase price, he had a considerable sum invested, and he took the only honorable method open to recoup part of the loss. He donated them to the National

Figures 152, 153, 154, & 155
Four of the famous Mt. Pisgah fake "Early Man" effigies of the late 19th century. Identification isn't easy, but these seem to include a group of three bears, a bear or tapir?, a Bactrian camel, and a whale?. *Courtesy the Valentine Museum.*

Park Service for use in connoisseurship classes and took a tax deduction for a portion of his costs.

In some situations there is not even the faint hope of legal redress. This applies to estate sales and public auctions where the terms of sale state that all transactions are final. Reputable auction houses catalog objects as accurately as they can, and some galleries have highly qualified experts on their staffs, but even the best of authorities make a mistake now and then. An individual dealer or a private seller may well state that all sales are final or he may have died or gone out of business between the time of your purchase and the moment of your disenchantment.

In these cases the response is up to your conscience. Many public institutions and organizations are happy to have fakes for instructional purposes—if they have not already found enough in their own collections. You can offer the fake to such a recipient and take a reasonable tax deduction. The amount of the deduction must be satisfactory to the tax officials, however, and the savings can never equal your actual investment. You can sell the piece honestly as a reproduction or fake at a fair price. There are a surprising number of people and dealers who will buy such items for their decorative quality or other utilitarian purposes. Or, if you have some doubts about whether the piece is genuine or not, you can offer it to an auction house and let the cataloger there decide how to describe it. No major auction house will accept a single obvious fake for sale, but even large museums have been known to mix very questionable pieces among other surplus objects and put them up for sale while positively disclaiming any responsibility for the attributions or descriptions that may appear in the sale catalog. Often, of course, you cannot be sure that a piece is spurious. You just know that you are unhappy with it, and in such cases it may be best to let someone else describe it and the public decide what price it should bring. After all, you might be wrong.

We won't even consider the final possibility: to say nothing

Figures 156 A & B (right)
Billy and Charley lead sculpture of a knight, c. 1850's. Like all the products of William Smith and Charles Eaton and their imitators, he resembles nothing of any period or area. *Collection of Claude Blair.*

Figure 157
Probably the biggest Billy and Charley known, this lead wine jug (?) stands 16½ inches tall. It is so heavy that the fragile handle broke years ago—and the vessel was empty.

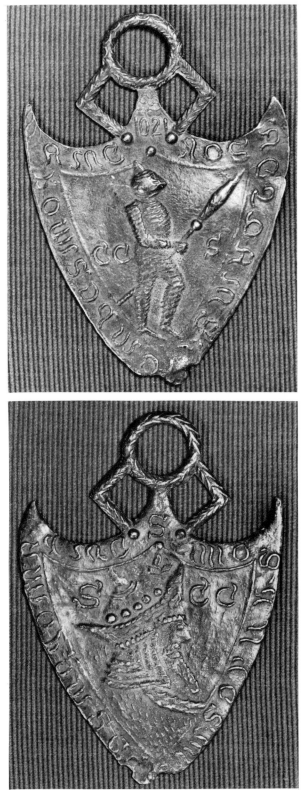

Figures 158 A & B
Front and back views of a Billy and
Charley medallion. Presumably the squiggles around the edges were intended to indicate an inscription in an ancient language, but the date of 1021 is clearly legi-
ble. The naïveté is marvellously intriguing.

and pass the monster on to someone more gullible. I have heard, however, that this has been done.

COLLECTING FAKES

Did I say "final possibility"? That's not quite correct. There is one other: you can start collecting fakes. Strange as this may sound, it is done. Personally, I find creative and ingenious fakes a fascinating field, and I buy them regularly if the price is right. I have, in fact, described myself as "a collector of fakes, some of which I've bought intentionally."

Famous fakes have always maintained a market among collectors. If the skull of Piltdown Man ever came on the market, I'm sure it would fetch a substantial price. So would the handsome "Etruscan" warriors once proudly exhibited at the Metropolitan Museum of Art. But there are lesser fakes that have extensive appeal. One collection of four spurious Colt revolvers, the so-called "Paterson-Walker" or "Edgerly" Colts which were invented in their entirety by the hoaxer have been offered in the catalog of one of the world's leading dealers in antique arms—as fakes, complete with a book written to prove their authenticity and documents exposing them—for $2,750!

Another type of fake that is exceptionally collectible might be typified by the so-called Mt. Pisgah sculptures. Their story is interesting for a number of reasons. In the middle of the last century the remarkable Richmond citizen Mann S. Valentine and his sons began an important collection of all manner of cultural materials, including archeological artifacts from Virginia and North Carolina. At one point in their collecting they acquired some fascinating animal effigies from the Mt. Pisgah area of North Carolina. At that time archeologists toyed with the idea that an "Early Man" culture preceded the appearance of the American Indian and that these ancient people had built the mounds of the Southeast where such effigies occasionally turned up. The Valentines promptly hastened to Mt. Pisgah, located a promising mound and attempted to purchase it. The farmer owner refused to sell. The Valentines asked if they could purchase rights to excavate the mound. Again the farmer refused. In desperation the ardent collectors then showed him their newly acquired effigies and asked that if he ever found figures of that sort on his land they might have a chance to buy them. The farmer agreed, and over the next few years he and his sons "found" quantities of the charming effigies. The Valentines bought scores of them. Others found their way into the collections of major museums in America and abroad. Everything was going beautifully. Collectors were delighted, scientists were intrigued, and the farmer and his family were prospering until one of the sculptors got carried away and carved a hippopotamus! That ended the dream, and the Mt. Pisgah effigies found themselves in museum attics, basements or dumps. In the 1950's the Valentine Museum sold some of its effigies very cheaply as fakes. Fortunately they did not sell them all. Now these delightful statuettes are recognized as exceptionally fine examples of 19th-century folk sculpture, and the Museum is planning a special exhibition of them for the near future. They have esthetic validity in their own right as well as a fascinating history.

Another highly collectible group of fakes are the famed "Billy and Charleys." Their origin is somewhat similar to the Mt. Pisgah effigies. During construction of the new dock on the Thames at Shadwell workmen reportedly found ancient artifacts which eager antiquarians quickly gathered up. Some of these objects may have been genuine, but many were dreadful fakes. Sales had been so good that a deluge of false antiquities descended upon the London market. Two workmen living in Rosemary Lane, Tower Hill, who were known then and now as Billy and Charley entered into the spirit of things so wholeheartedly that all the lead and cockmetal (an alloy of lead and copper) fakes of this period are named after them. Actually Billy and Charley worked in other materials as well and at least some of the metal products were probably made by competitors. No matter, the extent of production was prodigious. They made coins, pilgrim medals, plaques, vessels of various kinds, statuettes *ad infinitum*. H. Syer Cuming, who helped expose their activities in a presentation to the British Archaeological Association, claimed to have examined over 800 examples of their work, and he probably saw only a portion of it. Specimens still turn up today in London shops and in stalls of the Bermondsey Market and the Portobello Road, even in historic houses open to the public.

Looking at them today, one can hardly understand how anyone could have been taken in. Billy and Charley had no knowledge of period design, of dress, ancient languages or even of Middle English. Some have suggested that they were almost completely illiterate. As a consequence their creations are full of anachronisms, meaningless groups of letters or just squiggles that suggest no real letter or character in any language. The metal is illogical for the use intended—in those instances when you can guess what that intended use might have been. In short they are just about as naive a group of fakes as anyone could imagine.

Perhaps it is this very naivete that makes them attractive to collectors today. They are a curiosity and a delight to exhibit when one speaks patronizingly about how easily old-time collectors could be taken in. For whatever reason, Billy and Charleys are now much in demand. Recently, when I wrote a colleague at the Victoria & Albert Museum in London for some photographs of their collection of these fakes, he kindly complied, but added in his letter: "You will be interested to know that in the past year I have seen several fake Billy and Charleys." So now it appears we must learn to separate the genuine fake from the fake fake, and that is a good place to stop.

Guide to Further Reading

Many books have short sections on forgeries in their fields, but the following volumes deal entirely with fakes. In selecting the titles listed below I have eliminated those that are entirely anecdotal or deal exclusively with the field of fine arts or documents.

J. Duncan Campbell, *New Belt Buckles of the Old West,* Harrisburg, Pennsylvania, 1973.
  Colonel Campbell, Director of the William Penn Memorial Museum and a longtime student of belt buckles, thoroughly exposes the host of fake Wells Fargo, Cola-Cola, prison guard, Columbian Exposition and other late 19th-century style buckles that have recently flooded the market. In so doing he also demolishes a fraudulent book published in an attempt to prove them genuine. It is a fascinating detective story as well as an invaluable guide.

Herbert Cescinsky, *The Gentle Art of Faking Furniture,* London, 1931, reprinted New York, 1967.
  The old classic in the field with its primary emphasis on English furniture, this volume still presents a philosophical approach to the examination of artifacts that has never been superseded.

W. Crawley, *Is It Genuine? A Guide to the Identification of*

Eighteenth-Century English Furniture, London and New York, 1971.

The subject is even more narrowly circumscribed than the title indicates, for the author discusses only high style English 18th-century furniture, principally that produced in London. Since the author was himself a cabinet maker who admits to having produced a few pieces that have since been accepted as antique and to have altered many others, this volume offers some very interesting discussions of techniques and clues. Many of his assertions, however, are overly dogmatic. It is doubtful if all of them are universally true for London furniture of the era. Many would certainly not hold true for provincial or American furniture.

Dorothy Hammond, *Confusing Collectibles,* Leon, Iowa, 1969.

This is a very good survey of the reproductions currently on the market, with especial emphasis on 19th-century ceramics. It is a fine pictorial reference.

Charles H. Hayward, *Antique or Fake?,* London and New York, 1970.

A cabinet maker who learned his trade at the turn of the century when traditional methods were still employed, the author presents an exceptionally good guide to constructional clues in the detecting of fakes in furniture.

Ruth Webb Lee, *Antique Fakes & Reproductions,* enlarged and revised edition, Wellesley Hills, Massachusetts, 1950.

Although this volume is primarily devoted to forgeries of American glass, there are also some useful comments on fakes in other fields. The emphasis is on failures in design and style.

The Minneapolis Institute of Arts, *Fakes and Forgeries,* Minneapolis, Minnesota, 1973.

A catalog of a special exhibition on the subject, this heavily illustrated volume places its prime emphasis on the fine arts. A number of objects illustrated and described, however, fall within the categories discussed in this book. The descriptions are good and the pictures excellent. It should be noted, however, that in a couple of instances the captions appear to have been switched so that the fake is identified as the original.

E. Andrew Mowbray, editor, *Arms—Armor from the Atelier of Ernst Schmidt, Munich,* with an introduction by Stephen V. Grancsay, Providence, Rhode Island, 1967.
A photographic survey of the offerings of one of the most productive manufacturers of reproduction arms, armor and other military regalia who worked from 1868 until the 1930's, this volume offers a visual warning about many such objects now offered as genuine.

Robert Munro, *Archaeology and False Antiquities,* London, 1905.
This is the first book of its type in modern times. Most of it is anecdotal rather than technical, but it provides a good basic philosophical approach to the study of antiquities.

Riccardo Nobili, *The Gentle Art of Faking,* London, 1922.
This is a history of faking, mostly in the field of European fine arts, but some of the author's generalizations have a broader application.

Adolf Rieth, *Archeological Fakes,* translated from the German by Diana Imber, London, 1970.
Although it is primarily anecdotal in nature, this small volume offers some technical clues for detecting fakes in its field. It also presents a good cross-section of the types of fakes often encountered. The translation of technical terms is not always precise.

George Savage, *Forgeries, Fakes & Reproductions,* New York, 1964.
The emphasis is primarily European and heavily on the fine arts. There are very few illustrations, but comments on manufacturing techniques are very helpful.

N. H. Winchell, "The Weathering of Aboriginal Stone Artifacts

No. 1, A Consideration of the Paleoliths of Kansas," *Collections* of the Minnesota Historical Society, XVI, Part 1, St. Paul, Minnesota, 1913.

The author is primarily concerned with proving a thesis about the date of certain stone implements, but his observations on weathering and patination on both European and American stone artifacts are useful guides to all students of stone implements.

Raymond F. Yates, *Antique Fakes and their Detection,* New York, 1950.

The author's primary purpose is to warn that fakes exist and to indicate dishonest business practices. The strongest sections relate to wood and the hardware found on furniture.

INDEX